EUROPE'S MYTHS OF ORIENT

EUROPE'S MYTHS OF ORIENT

Devise and Rule

Rana Kabbani

MACMILLAN

First published 1986

Published by
THE MACMILLAN PRESS LTD
Houndmills, Basingstoke, Hampshire RG21 2XS
and London
Companies and representatives
throughout the world

Typeset by
Wessex Typesetters,
Frome, Somerset

Printed in Hong Kong

British Library Cataloguing in Publication Data
Kabbani, Rana
Europe's Myth's of Orient
1. Public opinion—Europe   2. Islamic
countries—Foreign opinion, European
I. Title
909'.097671   DS35.7
ISBN 0–333–37046–5

01372017

For Samia and Ali

Contents

List of Plates

Acknowledgements

The author and publishers wish to thank the following who have kindly given permission for the use of copyright material: Gillon Aitken and Alfred A. Knopf Inc. for extracts from *An Area of Darkness* and *Among the Believers* by V. S. Naipaul; from *The Voices of Marrakesh*, A Record of a Visit by Elias Canetti. English translation copyright © 1978 by Marion Boyars Publishers Ltd. Reprinted by permission of The Continuum Publishing Company; Curtis Brown Ltd and Viking Penguin Inc. for an extract from *Arabian Sands* by Wilfred Thesiger; Jonathan Cape Ltd., and Doubleday and Co. Ltd., for an extract from *Seven Pillars of Wisdom* by T. E. Lawrence. Every effort has been made to trace all the copyright holders but if any have been inadvertently overlooked the publishers will be pleased to make the necessary arrangement at the first opportunity.

I am deeply indebted to Adrian Poole, Lisa Jardine, Garth Fowden and Norman Bryson for having read this work in all its stages and for all the kindness they showed me during the writing of it.

This book could not have been completed without the generous support of the British Council, the Overseas Research Students Awards Scheme and the Akram Ojjeh Educational Foundation. I am grateful to them all for their assistance.

Rana Kabbani

'It is only natural that they insist on measuring us with the yardstick that they use for themselves, forgetting that the ravages of time are not the same for all, and that the quest of our own identity is just as arduous and bloody for us as it was for them. The interpretation of our reality through patterns not our own serves only to make us ever more unknown, ever less free, ever more solitary.'

Gabriel Garcia Marquez
'The Solitude of Latin America'

Introduction

I can never romanticize language again
never deny its power for disguise
for mystification
but the same could be said for music
or any form created
painted ceilings beaten gold
worm-worn Pietàs reorganizing victimization
frescoes translating violence
into patterns so powerful and pure
we continually fail to ask are they true for us.

Adrienne Rich,
A Wild Patience Has Taken Me This Far

The idea of travel as a means of gathering and recording information is commonly found in societies that exercise a high degree of political power. The traveller begins his journey with the strength of a nation or an empire sustaining him (albeit from a distance) militarily, economically, intellectually and, as is often the case, spiritually. He feels compelled to note down his observations in the awareness of a particular audience: his fellow-countrymen in general, his professional colleagues, his patron or his monarch. Awareness of this audience affects his perception, and influences him to select certain kinds of information, or to stress aspects of a country that find resonances in the culture of his own nation. His social position also colours his vision, and (since he often belongs to a leisured class, which enables him to embark on voyages which are both expensive and prestigious) he usually represents the interests and systems of thought in which he was schooled.

The traveller who sets out from a strong nation to seek out curiosities in lands less powerful than his own is to be found in many different civilisations.[1] The Islamic world, for instance, from the seventh to the fourteenth centuries composed of military and political powers which held sway over an area that came to stretch from Spain to China, sent out travellers, either as emissaries or as explorers, to bring back knowledge that could be used to enrich the store of politically useful information. As the Arabs grew more powerful, the number of travel books in their literature increased accordingly.[2] These found a receptive audience, since they conveyed information both about the Arabs' own dominions and about areas outside their empire which were of economic importance to them. Arab travellers and geographers took a strong interest in economic history, since the Arabs travelled primarily for purposes of trade. But the travel narrative also produced an ethnological discourse, of great relevance to the empire since it offered information about the peoples ruled.

As the Caliphate expanded and the power of the central authority became more fragile, there arose a desire to know in order the more effectively to rule.[3] But the travelogue also included more fanciful information, exaggerating or inventing accounts of distant lands for the sake of pleasing the reader. Travellers depended on each other's testimony in order to forge a communal image of the lands in which they travelled. They quoted each other in their accounts, as for example Mas'udi and al-Sirafi did,[4] and breathed new life into old stories that would otherwise have passed out of currency. Thus Idrisi, writing about South-East Asia in the twelfth century, incorporated material which was by then three hundred years old.[5] And although most of the travellers who wrote were increasingly learned and careful, aspiring, like Abu Zaid al-Sirafi, to avoid the distortions prevalent in the accounts of sailors and merchants,[6] they could not help confirming certain myths to which their countrymen had grown accustomed.

One of the mythical realms that Arab geographers and travellers described was that of *Waq waq*, a land that came to be associated with different geographic locations, most often with Japan. Ibn Khurdadbih, writing in the ninth century, saw it as a land of conspicuous wealth:

> East of China is a country called Waq waq, which is so rich in gold that the natives manufacture with this metal chains for their dogs and collars for their monkeys. They sell tunics

embroidered with gold. One finds there ebony of excellent quality.[7]

Al-Maqdisi thought *Waq waq* was a region in India, so named because it produced trees whose fruit had mouths that cried: 'Waq! Waq!'[8] Thus the travellers who wrote such descriptions, often depending on hearsay or on their own creative suppositions, came to regard 'this name as referring to a country just beyond their reach in the general direction of the east'.[9] And as they explored new ground, *Waq waq* slowly receded, always to be the last unexplored island just over the eastern horizon.

Descriptions of distant lands peopled by fantastic beings have universally abounded, as one dominant group became able to forge images of the 'alien' by imposing its own self-perpetuating categories and deviations from the norm. Pliny's *Natural History*, with its numerous entries on the customs of Anthropophagi, Astomi (who lived by smelling apples), Gymnosophists, Sciopods, Amazons and Brahmins, provides an early example of ethnocentric discourse. Consequently, the popularity of Pliny's work in medieval Europe lay mainly in the fact that it catalogued the beliefs about obscure races prevalent until then: an intellectual *mappa mundi* of sorts, it reinforced and reiterated current *idées reçues*. In the same manner, medieval and renaissance travel accounts as a genre came to depict voyages of a deliberate and self-conscious strangeness as they catered to the needs of sedentary audiences desiring depictions of the extraordinary.

The persona of the traveller, whether merchant like Marco Polo or sailor like Pigafetta, imposed itself with considerable force on the popular imagination. He introduced horizons, negotiated with alien cultures, solidified the data of geographical and ethnographical enquiry, and was the agent of the superior civilisation. He came to be a chronicler of conquest and conversion also. Describing Magellan's voyage of the early sixteenth century, Pigafetta wrote in a strain that would be echoed by nineteenth-century colonialism:

That day we baptised eight hundred persons, men, women, and children. The queen was young and beautiful, covered with a white and black cloth. She had a very red mouth and nails, and wore on her head a large hat made of palm leaves.[10]

The encountered natives had somehow to be converted, controlled. The Calibans of the New World, they were tolerable only when subdued. In order to justify such servitude forced upon a people, this kind of narrative stressed the conspicuous cruelty, the lechery, or the perversity of the natives. It was thus that Columbus cultivated the theme of cannibalism as he urged Spain to enter into slave-trading, or Cortes depicted in graphic detail the sacrificial rites of the Mexicans to exonerate those measures he saw fit to take against them. Such a narrative reads differently, however, when compromised by the fact that between the years 1494 and 1504, three million South Americans died as a result of Spanish 'pacification'.[11]

The forging of racial stereotypes and the confirmation of the notions of savagery were vital to the colonialist world view. In colonial America, for instance, there was a systematic attempt to portray the Indian as an abductor of women, a killer of children, and a collector of scalps, as an apology for white brutality against him.[12] Thus as late as 1896, Theodore Roosevelt could write: 'The settler and the pioneer have at bottom had justice on their side; this great continent could not have been kept as a game preserve for squalid savages.'[13]

Having realised his possession of territory, the white man could afford to wander from the fixed notion of the evil native. The twin vagaries of American guilt and European Romanticism blended to produce a 'Noble Savage'; the discrepancy remained, however, between such an imaginative portrayal of the Indian, and the extermination he was faced with in real life. The savage was noble if he belonged to a dying species: the last of the Mohicans is majestic precisely because he *is* the last of the Mohicans. And Fennimore Cooper's magnanimity, as befits this particular narrative tradition, is limited; the Indians, if occasionally noble, are barbaric and blood-thirsty at large. In one episode, they are almost cannibalistic:

> The flow of blood might be likened to the outbreaking of a torrent; and as the natives became heated and maddened by the sight, many among them kneeled to the earth, and drank freely, exultingly, hellishly, of the crimson tide.[14]

The savage could sometimes win favour if he aided the white man in the latter's attempt to dominate the environment, as Friday aided Robinson Crusoe. The persona of Pocahontas, for instance, fulfils the role of the good native, since she forsakes her people and renounces her royal stature in order to save a white man. She is submissive, self-effacing and subject to conversion: from Indian princess, she is transformed into dutiful Christian wife. Her 'incorporation' into white society is meant to belie suspicions of that society's inhumanity, and also to appease its conscience.

The projection of evil onto marginal or powerless groups within a society has always been a convenient method of producing scapegoats. Medieval Europe, for example, tried Jews for a medley of mythic crimes: poisoning wells, killing children for their blood, crucifying victims, and eating them too.[15] By the same token, women were associated with the devil, and seen as enemies of the Church and civilisation.[16] This went to justify the witch-hunts that tried women for sexual rapaciousness, cannibalism, consorting with evil spirits, and being generally intractable and capricious.[17]

The projection of evil onto a faraway culture was also a significant aspect of medieval Europe's bulwark of bigotry. And since it had a portentous opponent in the Islamic state, it fashioned a polemic to check whatever influence such a rival state might have. This polemic was highly charged with hostility, and notable for the fanaticism that engendered it. Islam was seen as the negation of Christianity; Muhammad as an imposter, an evil sensualist, an Antichrist in alliance with the Devil. The Islamic world was seen as Anti-Europe,[18] and was held in suspicion as such. Christian Europe had entered a confrontation with the Islamic Orient that was cultural, religious, political and military, one that would decide from then on the very nature of the discourse between West and East. Post-Crusader Europe would never wholly emerge from the antagonism its 'Holy Wars' had plunged it into. Its old desire to assert itself against its Islamic rival converted easily into a determination to dominate; this would become the psychological motivation of imperialists from Napoleon onwards. In precisely this spirit, the French general Gouraud entered Damascus in 1920: he proceeded immediately to the tomb of Salah al-Dîn al-Ayoubi, who had defeated the Europeans in the Third Crusade, and announced gloatingly: 'Nous revoilà, Saladin!'[19]

In the European narration of the Orient, there was a deliberate stress on those qualities that made the East different from the

West, exiled it into an irretrievable state of 'otherness'. Among the many themes that emerge from the European narration of the Other, two appear most strikingly. The first is the insistent claim that the East was a place of lascivious sensuality, and the second that it was a realm characterised by inherent violence. These themes had their significance in medieval thought, and would continue to be voiced with varying degrees of forcefulness up to the present time. But it was in the nineteenth century that they found their most deliberate expression, since that period saw a new confrontation between West and East – an imperial confrontation. If it could be suggested that Eastern peoples were slothful, preoccupied with sex, violent, and incapable of self-government, then the imperialist would feel himself justified in stepping in and ruling. Political domination and economic exploitation needed the cosmetic cant of *mission civilisatrice* to seem fully commendatory. For the ideology of empire was hardly ever a brute jingoism; rather, it made subtle use of reason, and recruited science and history to serve its ends. The image of the European coloniser had to remain an honourable one: he did not come as exploiter, but as enlightener. He was not seeking mere profit, but was fulfilling his duty to his Maker and his sovereign, whilst aiding those less fortunate to rise toward his lofty level. This was the white man's burden, that reputable colonial *malaise*, that sanctioned the subjugating of entire continents.

Nineteenth-century Britain produced a growing mass of travel literature, in a frenzied attempt to know the world it was in the process of conquering. The travellers travelled for their *pâtrie*, as it were; they were the seeing eye, and the recounting voice. They often had financial backing from officialdom, since their travelogues ultimately served to forge the imperial representation of the world.

Although the eighteenth century had also produced a travel literature of some scope, it remained a genre that offered instruction of anecdotal quality only. Neoclassical taste dictated to a large extent what the eighteenth-century traveller could say.[20] He observed the generic convention of descriptive rather than autobiographical narrative. Wary of being dubbed a 'vain' traveller (as Sterne's Yorick had put it), he avoided delineations of the self and gave detailed accounts of the scenery instead. Like William Combe's Dr Syntax, he went in search of the Picturesque. The narrative he produced did not rival in ambitiousness its nineteenth-century counterpart, whose scope was imperial.

The nineteenth-century traveller was concerned with the scenery only as it served as backdrop for his progress. He was the journey's hero – not merely its narrator – and he spelled out his complacency, cherishing every opportunity to speak of the self. The *moi haissable* of classical sensibility was appropriately revamped to accommodate a Victorian glorification of individuals. The traveller was now Pilgrim and Hero and Christian Soldier; his reputation could quickly take on mythic proportions, as did those of Gordon and Lawrence. Indeed, any attempt to discredit him was viewed disfavourably as a transgression of sorts: Wilfrid Scawen Blunt's discriminating critique of Gordon's folly was badly received by his countrymen at large, who thought it recreant and even perfidious. After all, the mythic Self of the traveller contained the sum of what he transported – his education, emotions, biases and beliefs, laced with a strong dose of racial conceit, as befitted a century of imperialist travellers. Richard Burton was one of the most prolific among these, a staunch empire man through all his wayward wanderings. And significantly, it is his narrative that did most to asseverate the fiction of an erotic East. The Orient for Burton was chiefly an illicit space and its women convenient chattels who offered sexual gratification denied in the Victorian home for its unseemliness. The articulation of sexism in his narrative went hand in hand with the articulation of racism, for women were a sub-group in patriarchal Victorian society just as other races were sub-groups within the colonial enterprise. Oriental women were thus doubly demeaned (as women, and as 'Orientals') whilst being curiously sublimated. They offered a prototype of the sexual in a repressive age, and were coveted as the permissible expression of a taboo topic.

Although there were notable instances of Victorian women who travelled and wrote about the lands they passed through or took up residence in,[21] the very essence of Victorian travel writing remains an intrinsic part of patriarchal discourse, for it fed on and ultimately served the hierarchies of power. And although some women were bound to those hierarchies by birth or marriage, they remained token travellers only, who were forced by various pressures to articulate the values of patriarchy. Thus Isabel Burton's tomes were watered-down versions of her husband's works: she rewrote for the 'angel of the house' what he had produced for the gentleman's club.

Travel writing of the Victorian period was linked to the nascent discipline of anthropology. Although anthropology was later to become a leveller of cultures and races, its beginnings often served to bolster the self-esteem of the European by convincing him that he was the culmination of excellence in the human species. Other races were his inferiors, lower down on the great scale of being (how low depending on how dark they were). And since they were lower down on that chimerical scale, they shared many qualities with animals, of which unbridled sexual ardour was one. It is illuminating to note how often the native is compared to an animal in this narrative. Iago's reference to Othello as a 'Barbary horse' is only a foreshadowing of the more opprobrious epithets that the Victorians were to coin.

The gist of anthropological writing was shared by fiction as well as travel narrative. The self-conscious reinforcing of racial otherness was strikingly similar in these divergent genres. For example, Rider Haggard's classic, *King Solomon's Mines* (1885), which sold 30 000 copies in its first year of publication, and which was read by the public schoolboys who were to become the empire's administrators,[22] perpetuated all the crude stereotypes of primitive man, propounding the racial superiority of the Anglo-Saxon. Baden-Powell's vision of the Boy Scouts borrowed a great deal from anthropological descriptions of the initiation rites of primitive peoples (he had carefully read Fraser's *The Golden Bough*) in order to invent mock trials for European youths, who would naturally excel at overcoming them, given their innate superiority. Edgar Rice Burrough's Tarzan, King of the Jungle, is, after all, an aristocratic Anglo-Saxon; the Victorians could not be expected to lose their hearts to heroes of the wrong class, and race.

The traveller as hero was above all a survivor in all conditions. He could cross jungles, ford rivers, brave hordes of savages yet still retain his urbanity. Thus Stanley, meeting Livingstone at long last in the African wilderness, addressed him with the affectation of drawing-room decorum. He presumed, in his capacity as white man in the 'dark' continent, that his polite parlance, like his political power, would prevail over the rude environment.

The European in the East was preoccupied with his stature and status. He remained terrified of crossing racial barriers abroad as he had been of crossing class barriers at home. Afraid that he would somehow lose caste, he had to cling, as Norman Daniel has pointed out, to the idea that Westerners were intrinsically different from Easterners, in order to preserve intact the wholeness of the imperial myth.[23]

The colonies provided niches for misfits, for unruly or impoverished sons (of whom Clive and Burton were notable examples). Such men could rise to distinction and exercise power in the colonies in ways that would have been unimaginable in their own birthplaces. Thus the traditional fantasy about the East became linked to a new fantasy about the travellers themselves in the East. Kinglake's Oriental Grand Tour as described in *Eothen* is remarkable for its self-importance: he carries himself with the conceit of a master among servants throughout. The Oriental is a mere mental mummy[24] who is often entertaining, but always despicable. Indeed, Kinglake supposes him to be so servile that he grows in respect for the European who mistreats him:

> the Asiatic seems to be animated with a feeling of profound respect, almost bordering upon affection, for all who have done him any bold, and violent wrong, and there is always too, so much of vague, and undefined apprehension mixed up with his really well-founded alarms, that I can see no limit to the yielding, and bending of his mind when it is worked upon by the idea of power.[25]

One Oriental Governor whom Kinglake meets entertains great admiration for the English; this, the author tells his audience, is because he was once threatened with destruction by an English ship's captain.[26]

Often the travellers became the self-created heroes of the colonial world, who advocated firm rule in order to exorcise the phantom of their own insignificance. If they abased the natives, then their own stature would seem much greater by contrast. Burton's description of a Sindhi illustrated this attitude concisely:

> He is idle and apathetic, unclean in his person, and addicted to intoxication; notoriously cowardly in times of danger, and proportionately insolent when he has nothing to fear; he has no idea of truth or probity, and only wants more talent to be a model of treachery.[27]

Such descriptions could double as upper class perceptions of

England's lower classes. As V. G. Kiernan has stated, the racial
alien and the class alien were interchangeably offensive to
Victorian hierarchical thought: the 'discontented native in the
colonies', and the 'labour agitator in the mills, were the same
serpent in alternate guises'.[28]

In attempting to document the Orient (the Other, the opposite,
the enemy, the foil), as Edward Said has argued, the Occident
came to document itself.[29] Although the travel narrative of
Victorian England did reflect the personal idiosyncrasies of
individual travellers, it was mainly a recapitulation of inherited
ideas. It ultimately produced (with rare exceptions, of which the
writings of W. S. Blunt were one) a communal image of the East,
which sustained a political structure and was sustained by it. The
ideology of this political structure whilst forming itself can be
talked about as taste, as the dominant culture. This is not to say
that *all* travellers discussing the East misrepresented it, but that
the dominant misrepresentations were, unfortunately enough, the
ones that captured the public imagination in the West. The
travelogues were, after all, part of the Orientalism that abetted
empire. Curzon referred to Orientalist studies as the 'necessary
furniture' of empire, and no doubt they were precisely that. Power
has always needed knowledge, but it is not necessarily coercive or
in control all the time. It more often licenses and chooses, offering
benefaction here, patronage there. Thus, European culture came
to be framed by warped representations of the East – since in the
end the dominant taste and mythologising instinct triumphed.

To write a literature of travel cannot but imply a colonial
relationship. The claim is that one travels to learn, but really, one
travels to exercise power over land, women, peoples. It is a
commonplace of Orientalism that the West knows more about the
East than the East knows about itself; this implies a
predetermined discourse, however, which limits and in many
ways victimises the Western observer. It is as if the imagination of
the traveller, in order to function, has to be sustained by a long
tradition of Western scholarship, by other Western texts. This
makes for some antiquated metaphors and archaic concepts to
which the Western traveller is nevertheless inescapably
subservient. Thus, Chateaubriand, before embarking on his
pilgrimage to Jerusalem, prepared himself by reading 'à peu près
deux cents relations modernes de la Terre-Sainte'; he had *made* the
journey before ever having set foot outside of France. Yet this

condition of literary and cultural dependence reduces the Orient to a literary cliché. Chateaubriand finds himself weighed down by the heaviness of the Orientalist tradition on actually *arriving* àt Jerusalem. He feels acutely the limitations of the inherited language:

> Ici j'éprouve un véritable embarras. Dois-je offrir la peinture exacte des Lieux Saints? Mais alors je ne puis que répéter ce que l'on a dit avant moi: jamais sujet ne fut peut-être moins connu des lecteurs modernes, et toutefois jamais sujet ne fut plus complètement épuisé.[30]

If the language of ordinary description has been overworked and overburdened, then the only outlet is figurative language, the substitution of metaphor and reverie. The Orient becomes a pretext for self-dramatisation and differentness; it is the malleable theatrical space in which can be played out the egocentric fantasies of Romanticism. It affords endless material for the imagination, and endless potential for the Occidental self. That self was many-faceted in the Orient; it could be omnipotent like Napoleon, aggressively patriotic like Kinglake, pedantically studious like Lane, fiercely outrageous like Burton, or unabashedly licentious like Gide. In order for the Orient to continue to provide the Occident with such wealth of personas to choose from, it must remain true to itself, in other words, truly Oriental. If it diverged at all from its given Orientalness, it became useless, a travesty of what it was *supposed* to be. Indeed, the fact that it was actually peopled by natives (rather than an empty theatre for the Westerner's benefit) was in itself annoying. David Roberts, who painted idealised landscapes of Classical ruins, but who detested the Arabs whose forms littered the otherwise perfect scene, expressed his frustration in the following manner:

> Splendid cities, once teeming with a busy population and embellished with temples and edifices, the wonder of the world, now deserted and lonely, or reduced by mismanagement and the barbarism of the Muslim creed to a state as savage as wild animals by which they are surrounded. Often have I gazed on them till my heart actually sickened within me.[31]

The hostility to Islam and to Muslims was an integral part of most of the travellers' mental makeup. James Elroy Flecker, whose image of Araby still retains a powerful hold on the popular imagination, wrote: 'I hate the East – the Lebanon is Christian thank God – but I have written . . . the best Eastern poems in the language.' The imagination and the reality were obviously two very different things in the Western mind.

It was thus that the 'Orient' fulfilled those many needs that the European brought to it. The word itself evoked so many instant epithets (Saracen, imposter, Arabian Nights, desert, dance, odalisque, Crusade, Bible), that it took a very determined and collected mind to be able to see beyond such sensationalist surplus to the starker reality in question. Obviously enough, not all the representations that resulted were pernicious. There were some European minds that could perceive the common humanity in East and West. W. S. Blunt was such a mind, a staunch defender of Eastern rights against his own nation. Many painters, like Fromentin, Renoir and Matisse, were exhilarated by the Orient, and were therefore considerably enriched as artists by it. Although there was a determination on the part of the West to record all aspects of the Orient in order to facilitate its colonial designs, there was, at the same time, a genuine and disinterested interest on the part of some individuals in the different reality which the Orient seemed to them to be. Such individuals contributed to an immense expansion of human knowledge, and were not handicapped by the perceptions they had inherited.

The positive achievements of the travellers have been thoroughly studied and as often praised in both West and East. But I believe that room must be allowed for a critique of their prejudices and misconceptions. They were, after all, only human, and highly susceptible to the influence of their societies. Since this is not an historical survey of all the travel literature about the Near East (that task has been already accomplished by various scholars), I have been selective rather than exhaustive in my choice of texts. The concentration on Galland, Lane, Burton, Doughty and Lawrence was due to my belief that these particular writers were more influential than others in forming the West's attitude to the East in the nineteenth and twentieth centuries. I have, above all, concentrated my discussion on the makings of a literary Orient – the forming of a mythology with lasting influence.

In reading in and around this subject, I have come to feel very strongly indeed that in order to arrive at a West–East discourse liberated from the obstinacy of the colonial legacy, a serious effort has to be made to review and reject a great many inherited representations. For these inherited representations are so persistent, and so damaging (they are continually being reinvested with new life, as I have attempted to prove in my last chapter on contemporary travel narrative), that they cloud our urges to see beyond them, to our common humanity.

1 Lewd Saracens

THE POLEMIC IS FORMULATED

When in the third decade of the seventh century the newly Islamicised armies of Arabia launched their assault on Byzantium,[1] they struck a fatal blow at the Mediterranean fulcrum around which the empires of Europe had turned. The Christian Church which had spanned that strategic coastline found itself powerless before the victorious armies of the Arabs. With Islam established as the dominant religion on its eastern and southern coasts, the Mediterranean gradually changed for Christian Europe, from being a channel of commercial and cultural intercourse into a barrier to movement of most sorts save the openly piratical. At this time also, the Carolingian empire was emerging, imparting new focus and a new sense of identity to the races of Northern Europe. Thus the Mediterranean came to be conspicuously remote to them, and the East seemed more and more to be the enemy.

The mental barrier between Christian Occident and Muslim Orient was upheld by ignorance and related myth-making. The West perceived the East as a dangerous region, where Islam flourished and monstrous races multiplied and thrived.[2] The Muslims were themselves seen as a monstrous race, and portrayed as black, dog-headed and ugly. There was a widespread association of Saracens and Cynocephali.[3] This hostility produced an anti-Islamic polemic, which made it 'possible to protect the minds of Christians against apostasy and . . . gave Christianity self-respect in dealing with a civilisation in many ways its superior'.[4]

One of the strategies of this polemic was to ridicule Muhammad in the most virulent manner possible. He was described as an arch-seducer, who wore purple, coloured his lips, and delighted in scented things and coition.[5] He was believed to have brought in

God to warrant his own sexual indulgences. Gerald of Wales, writing in the twelfth century, but reasoning in a manner that foreshadowed that of early nineteenth-century anthropology, thought Muhammad's teachings to be concentrated on lust, thus particularly suitable for Orientals, since they lived in a climate of great natural heat.[6]

One popular tradition attributed to Muhammad a plan for general sexual profligacy as an instrument for the destruction of Christianity.[7] Guibert of Nogent justified the inaccuracies prevalent in his biography of Muhammad by claiming that it was 'safe to speak evil of one whose malignity exceeds whatever ill can be spoken'.[8]

Medieval secular literature reflected the convictions of earlier religious polemic. The Muslims played a key role in the *chanson de gestes*, predictably as villains.[9] Thus the Saracens in the *Song of Roland* (who worship Antichrist, Lucifer, Termageunt and Diana among other idols) provide occasion for European heroics. They are there to be killed by the Christian knights.[10] *Piers Plowman* contains the common depiction of Muhammad as religious transgressor with infernal powers. And Dante relegates his Muhammad to that lowly circle in hell where the sowers of heresy go, to be constantly cleft in two for his crime.

In their portrayal of the alien Saracens, the Middle English Romances were essentially vehicles of propaganda, in which the ideals of chivalry became subservient to the requirements of religion and politics. As Dorothy Metlitzki has argued, 'the ideal held up to the audience is not courtly love or perfect knighthood. It is the triumph of Christianity of Islam'.[11] These Romances contained wish-fulfilling embodiments: the Saracen giant killed by a Christian hero, the defeated emir, the converted Saracen, and most importantly, the Saracen princess in love with the Christian knight.[12]

The Romance of *Sir Bevis of Hampton*[13] contains the prototype of the enamoured Saracen princess. She is ready to serve her knight with slavish devotion. He inspires ardent desires in her, and this because she is inherently lusty. Muslim princesses are the wooing women of medieval temptation scenes,[14] who walk unbidden into bedchambers and proffer their bodies only to be virtuously refused. These seductresses will even forsake their religion for love of the knight.[15] Josian swears to Sir Bevis that she will embrace

Christianity if he would only embrace her. He agrees with missionary zeal, and she becomes a 'good' Saracen when converted.

In the Romance of *The Sowdone of Babylone*,[16] Floripas is the Saracen princess who, for love of the knight imprisoned in her father's castle, forsakes her religion and deceives her relations. When her duenna, Maragounde, refuses to comply with her wishes to help the knight, Floripas pushes her out of a window and into the sea. And she is not only perfidious and murderous, but lascivious as well. Before aiding the knights to overpower her father in his own castle, she lures Guy of Burgundy into her chamber and proceeds to seduce him despite his valorous unwillingness. This theme is not unique to this particular Romance, for it represents a standard scenario in which Christian knights overpower a Saracen king with the help of his wife or daughter. What seems important in this framework is not the military defeat of the enemy but 'the degradation of the sultan or emir through the enmity and treachery of his own kin'.[17]

While the Muslim princess is represented as treacherous, lewd and selfish, the Christian heroine of the Romances is self-sacrificing and virtuous. In the Romance of *The King of Tars*,[18] a Christian princess, in order to save her people from destruction, resignedly agrees to marry a Saracen king who is portrayed as black and heathenish. When they are vexed with the misfortune of a deformed child, the mother is permitted to have it baptised. It immediately turns into a handsome and whole infant, so pleasing the Saracen king that he requests to undergo the same operation. He, too, is transformed by it, and turns white.

In the Romance of *Floris and Blauncheflur*[19] there is one of the earliest descriptions of a harem, guarded by eunuchs. Also described are merchants who supply the sultan with beautiful female slaves. It was in such ways that the East as a land that traded in voluptuousness, a land where sexual desires could be gratified to the hilt, acquired currency.

To support the idea of a voluptuous East, the West inflated the Quranic idea of Paradise, arguing that Muslims were not only lewd in every day life, but had conceived of a heaven that would permit endless sensual gratification, ignoring the fact that the Christian Paradise itself promised rivers, gardens, milk and honey. The notion of the carnal delights of the Islamic heaven was sharply contrasted, in an effort to mock it, with the angelic society of the Christian paradise. Christians were morally refined and longed for a bodiless heaven; Muslims were spiritually coarse and could not envisage bliss that was not corporeal.

Thus a pattern of stereotyping emerged that was a guarantee of Western self-respect and a projection upon the rest of the world of Western values. The medieval picture of Islam was replete with errors that were wilful, and contained within itself a high degree of mythomania. The 'we – they' dichotomy of European observation was supported by the testimony of fictive or real travellers such as Alexander,[20] Mandeville,[21] Marco Polo,[22] and Odoric.[23]

Renaissance England inherited the stereotyped image of the East from the Middle Ages, as it inherited the fear of the Saracens – now embodied in the Ottoman threat to Europe. From Classical sources (from Cicero and Horace) it revived the image of fabulous Eastern wealth. Ormuz, Ophir and Aleppo came to be synonymous with great riches in the mythology of a nation which was becoming more and more preoccupied with trade. The first fully-fledged trading expedition to Syria in 1583[24] is mentioned two decades later in *Macbeth*, a reflection of the importance such an event must have had:

> *1st Witch*: A sailor's wife had chestnuts in her lap
> And munched, and munched, and munched: 'Give me',
>   quoth I.
> 'Aroint thee, witch!' the rump-fed ronyon cries.
> Her husband's to Aleppo gone, master of the Tiger:
> But in a sieve I'll thither sail,
> And, like a rat without a tail,
> I'll do, I'll do, and I'll do.[25]

The antique notion of a rich East (confirmed by such traditions as the three Magi and the Queen of Sheba) is linked, in Elizabethan England, with eroticism. The luxury of wealth is associated with libidinousness and idleness. Easterners are seen as decadent languishers in rich harems, who do not exert themselves as do the energetic English.

One English woman who did exert herself to win the Turkish Sultan's favour in order to obtain trade concessions and military alliance was Queen Elizabeth. In 1598, Thomas Dallam, who had built an ornate organ for Her Majesty's pleasure, was instructed to accompany his handiwork to Constantinople, where it was to

be offered as a present to the Sultan. Dallam obliged, but was
greatly perplexed on landing in Turkey to find that his organ had
come unglued, on account of the 'hootness of the cuntrye'. Making
desperate amends, he managed to have it presented at Court, to
the delight of the Sultan who pressed him to remain at
Constantinople. Dallam's homesickness got the better of him,
however, and he decided to make his way back to England (where
he would build the organ for King's College, Cambridge), but not
before he managed a glimpse of the seraglio:

> When I came to the grate the wall was very thick, and grated on
> both sides with iron very strongly; but through that grate, I did
> see thirty of the Grand Sinyor's concubines that were playing
> with a ball in another court. At the first sight of them I thought
> they had been young men, but when I saw the hair on their
> heads hang down on their backs, plaited together with a tassel
> of small pearl hanging in the lower end of it, and other plain
> tokens, I did know them to be women, and very pretty ones
> indeed . . . I stood so long looking upon them that he which
> showed me all this kindness began to be very angry with me.
> He made a wry mouth, and stamped with his foot to make me
> give over looking; the which I was very loathe to do, for that
> sight did please me wondrous well.[26]

Such anecdotal accounts became the staple offering of travellers
who felt obliged to describe the seraglio for their compatriots'
entertainment. The descriptions were of a predictable similarity,
and reinforced each other to create a definitive edifice of sexuality
and despotism. This edifice became a metaphor for the whole
East, fulfilling as it did a bulk of European fantasy needs. These
descriptions were a self-perpetuating *topos*, repeated and copied
again and again since they corresponded exactly to Western
expectations.[27]

Travellers who described architectural aspects of the 'Grand
Turk's' Court could not resist adding details which made their
accounts more fabulous. Sir George Courthope, writing in the
mid-seventeenth century, peopled the empty gardens of the
palace grounds at Constantinople with the ready prototypes of
princes, eunuchs and naked concubines. Espying a pond made of
porphyry, he imagined the Sultan before it, engaged in titillating
games:

Here he putteth in his Concubines stark naked and shooteth at
them with certain pelletts that stick upon them without any
damage to their bodies. And sometimes he lets the water in such
abundance upon them . . . that being above their heights they
all bob up and down for life; and when his pleasure is satisfied
with the sport, he lets down the water, and calls the Eunuchs
who wait upon his women, to fetch them out if alive.[28]

Such scenarios summed up the East for the Western reader: a
sexual *lieu*, a despotic and capricious one to boot. Orientals could
do no better than indulge in such pastimes, for they were oblivious
of time, caught in a timeless self-indulgence.

The cruelty of the Oriental in narrative constructions went
hand in hand with his lasciviousness. One favourite example that
reappears with great frequency during this period is the story of
the Turkish Sultan who falls in love with a slave-girl, so that he
abandons all matters of state to lie in her embraces.[29] Rebuked by
his ministers and officers, who press him to attend to his army
about to engage in battle, he is only enraged at their meddling.
One evening, he bids his lover dress in her most revealing silks and
attend to him at a banquet. He embraces her before his courtiers,
then abruptly draws his sword and cuts off her head. Another
version has him bid his ministers into his bedchamber, where he
lifts the bedclothes to reveal to them the naked charms of his
mistress. This done, he stabs her to death, and marches off to war.

This constructed narrative was a corollary to Elizabethan
England's construction of a trade empire. For it was this period
that saw the foundations being laid for a later imperial entity, as
acquisitive merchants went far in converting piracy to patriotism
in their efforts to win markets further afield than home. These
commercial travellers were above all preoccupied with the details
of trade. But they did sometimes take an interest, if for reasons of
profit alone, in the peoples native to the countries they coveted.
The Levant Company, for instance, commissioned a report on
'the chief mart of all the East' – Aleppo – from one Charles
Robson.[30] Such accounts, however, did little to change inherited
notions of what the East was like. Travellers merely confirmed
that Easterners were fanatical, violent and lusty souls.

The Elizabethan stage, preoccupied as it was with the
melodramatic, the passionate and the violent, drew heavily on the
available stock of Eastern characters so vivid in the public

imagination.[31] The Saracen, the Turk, the Moor, the Blackamoor
and the Jew were key villains in the drama of the period, crudely
depicted as such by the lesser playwrights, but drawn with more
subtle gradations by a Marlowe or a Shakespeare. Although
Shakespeare 'whitewashes' Othello by making him a servant of
the Venetian state, a soldier fighting for a Christian power, and
most importantly, a killer of Turks, he still remains a savage –
although a somewhat noble one. His excitable nature and his
passionate instincts flaw him: his jealousy recalls a long tradition
of Eastern jealousy, his revenge a confirmed consequence of that
tradition. The play ultimately condemns the idea of inter-racial
sex, for such intercourse can only lead to tragedy, upsetting as it
does the fixedness of the *status quo*. The black man cannot simply
be allowed to 'tup' the 'white ewe' uncurbed; both must be
punished for such transgression, even when their mutual affection
draws a cautious amount of sympathy for them.

⎣The voyage to the Orient and the contact with the Oriental is
often tinged with danger.⏌Shakespeare's Mark Antony embarked
on that voyage a 'firm Roman', but as the play opens, he has been
captivated by its erotic possibilities, fallen into the lassitude of
love hours, fallen from his former stature – fallen, in short, into the
East (which is set as a foil to Rome). His dotage 'o'erflows the
measure', and his captain's heart has become 'the bellows and
the fan to cool a gypsy's lust'. If Rome connotes duty,
respectability, social position, empire and marriage, then Egypt
(Cleopatra being Egypt, and Egypt possessing Cleopatra's
powers of enchantment) is the indulgence of the senses, oblivion to
the world's affairs, and overwhelming sexual desire.

Antony is well aware of his state, and wishes to extricate himself
from passion ('I must from this enchanting queen break off'), but
knows that he must resolve the duality of needs within himself –
the need for statesmanship that the journey West offers, and the
desire for passion that the journey East requites. The Western tug
wins momentarily and he vows:

> These strong Egyptian fetters I must break,
> Or lose myself in dotage.[32]

But the choice resolves nothing, for as the journey West returns
Antony to all the things that Egypt had negated, he finds himself
once more desiring those powers of negation. He settles his score

with Caesar, re-enters the public arena, and contracts a political marriage. But as Caesar and Octavia leave the scene, Antony clarifies his intentions; he wishes to use both West and East to contain his needs. The soothsayer he encounters returns him to the circle of magic, of fortune-telling, of intuition that Egypt had represented for him, and reminded of desire, he says:

> I will to Egypt:
> And though I make this marriage
> For my peace,
> In the East my pleasure lies.[33]

The dichotomy has now crystallised: the West is social stability; the East pleasure, unrestricted by social dictates. Antony desires both, although of necessity preferring one to the other (since the two are mutually incompatible as this play suggests) at different moments of the drama. Even the dialogue of two onlookers confirms the unappeasable nature of these warring urges in Antony as they describe the two women who meet those urges. Maecenas stresses Octavia's 'wisdom, modesty' and her being a social boon to Antony, a 'blessed lottery to him', while Enobarbus dwells on the spectacle of Cleopatra in describing her approaching barge: 'She makes hungry where most she satisfies' – she is the sexual urge itself, unappeasable and intransigent.

The defeat comes when Antony can no longer keep separate West from East, duty from passion, war from *amor*. When Cleopatra leaves the battle at the decisive moment, Antony follows, 'the noble ruin of her magic'. He lives to regret it, and heap abuse on the object of love:

> O this false soul of Egypt!
> This grave charm
> Whose eyes becked forth my wars
> And called them home,
> Whose bosom was my crownet,
> My chief end—
> Like a right gypsy hath at fast
> And loose
> Beguiled me to the very heart of loss.
> What, Eros, Eros![34]

These two warring urges in Antony are only resolved in death, a loss of all, and a state that is almost stronger than passion – but not quite, since he dies kissing Cleopatra. In death the conflict ends, with East and West claiming his qualities as their own.

For Antony, the East arrived in Cleopatra's barge. It was a mixture of new delights: the pomp of pageant, the smell of perfume and incense, the luxurious brocades that shimmered in the sun, and most notably, the woman herself – queen, love-object, mistress and despot – *was* the East, the Orient created for the Western gaze.

The European retained a sense of sexual expectancy from the East, having encountered in both mythological and theological texts the prototype of the seductive Eastern woman. Virgil's Dido welcomes Aeneas into her bed as Cleopatra does Mark Antony. She is desire personified, conceived primarily as a love-object for the wandering hero, her royal stature only adding to her sexual desirability. She retains Aeneas in the tradition of all temptresses, and is lost when he regains his powers to depart. Fiery and unforgiving as she is, she can only revert to violent measures, and so lights the flames that consume her. Medea is violent too, carrying the extremes of passion in her which set her apart from the Attic, from the mean. She is different, other, Eastern, barbarian, and attracts and repels at the same time.

Balqis of Yemen is the Arab beauty to whom King Solomon addresses his most passionate words. She is the spark of the sexual narrative, bejewelled and exotic – fantasy's spouse. Salome's beauty and her wickedness are inseparable; her dance arouses as it horrifies. She becomes of particular iconic value in Renaissance painting, and again in late nineteenth-century painting, literature and music.

The Eastern woman was a narrative creation that fulfilled the longings of Western imagination; soon, that very imagination would be deeply stirred by an Eastern woman (being herself a creation) who created narrative as nebulous and as nocturnal as the Western listener could desire. In 1704, yet another prototype of Eastern sensuality perceived the day, and she took Europe by storm. Her name was Scheherazade.

'ARABIAN NIGHTS'

The collection of stories commonly referred to as the 'Arabian Nights'[35] was never a definitive text in Arabic literature as is generally supposed by a Western reader. These stories, the *Alf laila wa laila* "ملیﻟ و "ملیﻟ ﻒﻟأ were first and foremost folklore kept alive orally. They were narrated by itinerant *conteurs* or *hakawatieh*, who augmented their content, elaborated on their plot structures, and larded them with anecdotes or verses which reflected their respective tastes. Thus the stories came to be conspicuously diverse, differing quite markedly from version to version, and illustrating in this the singularities of each *hakawati*'s locale. They were narrated in the popular quarters along with the stock epics such as *'Antar*, or romances such as *Qais wa Leila*.

Emerging from the oral folkloric tradition central to India, Persia, Iraq, Syria and Egypt, these stories reflected the popular prejudices prevalent among the masses to whom they were recounted. Written in a vulgar vernacular to suit that audience, they could hardly be considered as cultivated literature. Indeed, they were relegated, in the rare instances when they were mentioned by historians or literary commentators, to the level of inferior entertainment. Al-Mas'udi first referred to them in that manner in *Muruj al-Dahab*, and Ibn al-Nadim, writing in the tenth century, considered them to be of no literary merit, but conceded rather disdainfully that they were popular among the illiterate.

When and why these stories were put into writing remains controversial, yet what appears clear is that they were recorded as a means of preservation, and that the manuscripts that resulted were as amorphous and diverse as the oral versions of the stories had been. Thus there was no definitive text of the *Alf laila wa laila*, but numerous variations on that particular sort of oral narrative. The versions that resulted were of different origins, belonged to different eras, and reflected the singularities of different geographical locations. It was only when a European encountered these stories, decided to translate them, and produced a set text that remained in currency for over a century (1704–1838) that they became institutionalised in the way they are known to the West.

The Frenchman Antoine Galland created a text out of the flexible material he had at his disposal. He is not a mere translator

of these Arabic stories; he is the inventor of a Western
phenomenon, a circular narrative that portrayed an imaginary
space of a thousand and one reveries. It was a marginal
manifestation of his career as scholar, but it was the work that won
him literary renown. He was his Scheherazade just as Flaubert
was his Emma Bovary.

Although it has been generally assumed that the *Arabian Nights*
were first introduced to the West in 1704 when Galland's first
volume was published, it can be safely conjectured that a great
many of these stories had been known in Europe as early as the
fifteenth century. Galland himself was aware of this early
acquaintance and of the literary borrowing that it engendered,
asserting that the tales were 'assez anciens, et la communication
qu'il y a eu de ces pays avec le Levant du temps des Croisades fait
que les auteurs de Vieux romans en ont tiré beaucoup de
choses'.[36] In France, for example, the Romance of *Cléomades*[37] rests
on themes remarkably similar to those of the 'Enchanted Horse'
story, and the Romance of *Pierre de Provence et la belle Maguelone*[38] is
almost identical to the story of 'Qamar al-Zamaan'. The
frame-tale of the *Arabian Nights* appears in Ariosto's *Orlando
Furioso*,[39] making quite certain Europe's familiarity with these
tales.

It remains unverifiable how these tales migrated as they did,
but it can be assumed that they were carried to Europe by
Christian and Jewish citizens of the Islamic dominions (by the
Spanish mozarebs, for instance), by returning Crusaders, by
travelling merchants or emissaries. The tales became yet another
commodity from the East, which circulated around the world like
the other commodities of spices and cloths,[40] and were exchanged
in humble sea-ports or in elegant *salons*.

Antoine Galland was an emissary of sorts, attached as he was to
the French diplomatic mission in Constantinople. The journal
that he kept during his sojourn there reflects his constant search
for and fascination with Oriental manuscripts. He seems to have
had a scholar's interest in perusing texts, as well as a collector's
prowess in bargaining to procure them.

Je vis un livre turc intitulé تذكرة الشعراء c'est à dire
Catalogue des poëtes. En effet il contenoit par ordre
alphabetiques les noms des plus fameux poëtes qui ont excellé
parmy les Turcs, avec leur éloge et le catalogue de leurs

ouvrages et un essay quelquefois de ce qu'ils ont fait de plus beau. Il estoit in folio et on l'estimoit dix piastres. On auroit pu l'avoir à moins de huit.[41]

Galland transcribed and translated many manuscripts from Turkish, Persian and Arabic.[42] He was continuing in the tradition of his teacher, d'Herbelot, a tradition of ambitious Orientalist erudition.[43] Indeed, when that latter died, leaving the mammoth *Bibliothèque Orientale* unfinished, it fell to Galland to complete it, and introduce it to the public.

Galland the scholar who had known the Levant only through its languages studied in France, became Galland the traveller who set down his observations of the newly-encountered world of Constantinople. Yet despite his scholarly carefulness, Galland could not help being seduced into seeing those aspects he had expected to see. Like many Europeans before him, he concentrated his attention on the manifestations of violence that were supposedly intrinsic to the East. One entry in his journal describes with macabre fascination (a macabre fascination that many Europeans felt for executions in Europe also during this period) the details of the execution of a band of thieves. The first thief is forced by the guard to say his prayers before he is clumsily decapitated:

> . . . on luy dit de faire sa prière et que tardant à la faire, on l'y avoit contraint à coups de baston; qu'ensuite s'estant mis à genoux à terre en caleçon, le bourreau le prit par le toupet de cheveux qu'il avoit au haut de la teste d'une main et luy donna le coup de l'autre, qu'il fût contraint de répéter n'ayant pas coupé la teste du premier. Il ne la coupa mesme pas entièrement du second; elle resta encor attachée à quelque filet de la peau. Le corps fût ainsy laissé estendu sur la place.[44]

The violence of the East was often linked in Galland's entries with sexuality. This was a common trope of European travel-writing: the all-invasive seraglio with its crimes of passion was never far from the traveller's mind. It was the most fascinating and the most disturbing image to him, and he devised endless means of portraying it. His descriptions served to elaborate upon those of previous travellers, sustaining as they did the same fictions.

Galland had been influenced by other European travellers to

the East. He had met Chardin, whose writings on Persia were instrumental in the forging of the eighteenth century's views of that part of the world. Although a sensitive and studious traveller, Chardin never managed to be an impartial one. He could not succeed in eluding the obligatory *topos* of the seraglio which Europe held so dear. Chardin emphasised the severity prevalent in the seraglio, enumerated the restrictions against women, provided examples of the capricious punishments that they were obliged to endure. He furnished his readers with anecdotes that summed up such strains. In one of these, Chardin recounts that King 'Abbas, much taken with a concubine, is asked by her to refrain from sex because she is indisposed. Suspicious of her excuse, he has the matter investigated, and finding her to be free from her 'incommodité de femme', he has her burnt alive.[45]

Such anecdotes helped keep in currency notions of a cruel and vengeful Eastern male (which become of vital importance in the Orientalist painting of the nineteenth century), the mephitic master who vilely abused his women. Galland recounts a story of a mistreated slave-girl made desperate by her keeper:

> Une esclave de Constantinople ayant été maltraitée de plusieurs coups de baston sur la plante des pieds par son patron, entra dans un désespoir si grand, qu'elle mit premièrement le feu dans la maison et se pendit ensuite, voulant ainsi punir la cruauté de son maistre et s'en affranchir en mesme temps.[46]

Europe's feelings about Oriental women were always ambivalent ones. They fluctuated between desire, pity, contempt and outrage. Oriental women were painted as erotic victims and as scheming witches. Chardin saw them as 'les plus méchantes femmes de la terre; fières, superbes, perfides, fourbes, cruelles, impudiques'.[47] They spent their lives in sexual preparation (Chardin recounted that they filled linen pouches with musk and introduced them 'dans la partie que la pudeur ne me permet pas de nommer'.[48]) and in sexual intrigue. They dallied with each other when their men were absent: 'les femmes Orientales ont toujours passé pour Tribades'[49] (a point that Burton would later stress[50]). They were lascivious and lazy – Chardin's summing up of their traits deserves quoting since it represented Europe's idea of Eastern womanhood:

elles passent leur vie dans la nonchalance, l'oisiveté, et la mollesse, étant tout le jour ou étendues sur des lits à se faire gratter et frotter par des petites esclaves, ce qui est une des plus grandes voluptez des Asiatiques, ou à fumer le Tabac du païs . . .[51]

It was such an idea that made Galland's fortune, since he happened upon the most fitting stories to feed it with.

Of all the translations that Galland made from Oriental languages in the course of a prolific academic career, only one attracted an enthusiastic welcome in Europe. *Les Mille et une nuits* was the least significant product of Galland's erudition; it was the least accurate as translation, and the least representative example of the literature he had studied, and with which he wished to familiarise his readers. He himself wrote of the stories in an unceremonious manner. He stressed the fact that he worked on them only after dinner, as a form of recreation to end a long day's more scholarly study.[52] When they met with instant success on publication, he was naturally flattered, although he realised, with a scholar's wounded self-esteem, the irony of his newly-acquired fame. He wrote to his friend Cuper that *Les Mille et une nuits*

sont assez bien reçus à la Cour, à Paris, et dans les Provinces, aussi bien par les Messieurs que par les Dames. On n'auroit pas le mesme empressement pour d'autres ouvrages que j'aurois pu faire imprimer il y a longtemps et qui ne le seront peut-être jamais.[53]

And yet Galland was not contemptuous of popular opinion. He had confessed to Cuper that he had wished to address a lay reader, to please rather than to instruct. He described his translation as one which was not 'attachée précisement au texte, qui n'auroit pas fait plaisir aux lecteurs. C'est autant qu'il m'a été possible, l'arabe rendu en bon françois, sans m'estre attaché servilement aux mots.'[54] In his effort to produce a pleasing text for his audience, Galland had curbed the Arabic vernacular to fit the exigent *preciosité* of eighteenth-century literary French. As an instance of this, he changed the simple Arabic lines in the 'Histoire du jeune roi des Iles Noires', in which the King bids his unfaithful spouse to cry until her grief has passed into the considerably more mannered response that follows:

Madame, lui dis je, loin de blâmer votre douleur, je vous assure que j'y prends toute la part que je dois. Je serais extrêmement surpris que vous fussiez insensible à la perte que vous avez faites: pleurez, vos larmes sont d'infaillibles marques de votre excellente nature. J'espère néanmoins que le temps et la raison pourront apporter de la modération à vos déplaisirs.[55]

Galland's rendering of the same tale reflected another characteristic of his method in general. He sought to bypass details that might have offended his readers by their unseemliness. Thus he omitted the description of sexual intercourse between the queen and her lover. In the frame-tale of the stories, when Shahzenan espies his brother's wife sleeping with her slave, Galland reverted to polite coyness, claiming that

La pudeur ne me permet pas de raconter tout ce qui se passa entre ces femmes et leurs noirs; il suffit de dire que Shahzenan en vit assez pour juger que son frère n'était pas moins à plaindre que lui.[56]

Such delicate censorship did not go unrewarded. For Galland's immortality was assured by the way Europe fell in love with *Les Mille et une nuits*. The apocryphal anecdote has it that in 1713, when there was a lull in his publication of further instalments of the tales, admiring crowds threw stones at his window at night, and called up to him: 'Monsieur Galland, si vous ne dormez pas, nous vous supplions, en attendant le jour qui paraitra bientôt, de nous raconter un de ces contes agréables que vous savez.'[57] These 'contes agréables' catered to the taste for *turqueries* prevalent in elegant society in Europe. The Orient as reflected in its imported literature became a decorative foil, a diverting contrast to the rationalism of the age. These stories met the eighteenth century's hankering after the primitive – that feigned simplicity inherent in Rousseau's back-to-nature call. Rousseau's Emile elevates Defoe's Crusoe above all other heroes, and it is interesting to discover that that adventure of shipwreck and desert-island heroics is modelled on the tale of Sindbad.[58]

Les Mille et une nuits, then, were greeted with great enthusiasm in an era that was fidgeting under the stern dominion of rationalism, desiring imaginative space and relief from sobriety. They came at a time of intellectual secularisation, when Europeans wished to become acquainted with cultures that were not Christian. The East was an obvious repository of such cultures, and although Islam continued to be regarded with suspicion and distaste,[59] its sublunary aspects as reflected in the *Les Mille et une nuits* produced a passionate desire for additional narrative of this kind. The disjunction remained, however, between the literary myth and the political fact. For Europe was already expressing relentless economic interest in the Orient, and the end of the eighteenth century would usher in the beginning of the imperialist presence there. Thus the fascination with a make-believe location was contiguous to the penetration of real Eastern markets.

The allure of *Les Mille et une nuits* led many Europeans to confuse the real East with the East of the stories. Lady Mary Montagu, for instance, believed the tales to be accurate descriptions of the Oriental society of which she found herself on the periphery in her capacity as British ambassador's wife. She wrote with endearing naïveté that these 'very tales were writ by an author of this country and (excepting the enchantments) are a real representation of the manners here.'[60] This confusion was partly due, as Leila Ahmed has suggested, to the numerous descriptions in the stories of real physical objects.[61] Thus it produced in the European reader's already susceptible imagination a strange 'sense of reality in the midst of unreality'.[62] Gobineau, travelling under this very influence, remarked that 'à chaque pas que l'on fait en Asie, on comprend mieux que le livre le plus vrai, le plus exact, le plus complet sur les royaumes de cette partie du monde, ce sont *Les Mille et une nuits*.'[63]

The phenomenon that came to be known popularly in England as the 'Arabian Nights' created a literary *frisson* that affected mainstream works of English (and more generally, European) fiction. The Orient of the stories became a convenient trope for poet and novelist, a metaphor that could express moral beliefs, or a frame-work for romanticism. Friedrich Schlegel summed up the Romantic movement's appreciation of the Orient's literary possibilities when he wrote:

> In the Orient we must look for the most sublime form of the Romantic, and only when we can draw from the source, perhaps will the semblance of southern passion which we find so charming in Spanish poetry appear to us occidental and sparse.[64]

The Romantics perceived the Orient as a world 'so different from the neo-classic, so unrationalistic, so coloured in its imaginative freedom, sensuousness and fatalism'.[65] It provided them with a set of hazy images, a *flou* landscape through which their heroes could move. Shelley's heroes (in *Alastor* and *The Revolt of Islam*, for example) visit ruins, voyage up the valley of the Nile, pass through Persia and Arabia, climb the Himalayas, arrive at the most solitary valley in Kashmir, illustrating thus the master theme of the major Romantic poems – the theme of travel.[66] Keats had put this desire into the following lines ('Sonnet to J. H. Reynolds'):

> O to arrive each Monday morn from Ind,
> To land each Tuesday from the rich Levant.

The Romantic's Orient was a sublimated location, with no connection to the real East. There was never any attempt to bring in a touch of urban scenery, nor was there ever a depiction of social misery. Poverty was conspicuously absent from this particular mythic Orient: riches took its place, and what Chateaubriand summed up as the 'bains, parfums, danses, délices de l'Asie'.[67]

One of the favourite Romantic themes was that of the nightingale and the rose, first brought into English literary awareness by Lady Montagu in her correspondence with Alexander Pope. She related in her letter of 1 April 1717, that the *bulbul* sang as sweetly as it did to describe its love for the rose. Such romantic allusions did not fall on deaf ears; Pope was only too pleased to pursue the Oriental theme in his courtship of Lady Montagu. Adopting the by then common trope of an erotic East, he wrote to her that she would soon be arriving 'in the Land of Jealousy, where the unhappy Women converse with but Eunuchs, and where the very Cucumbers are brought in Cutt'.[68] He would be following her progress, he continued, as she penetrated Eastward:

> At this Town, they will say, she practised to sit on the Sofa; at that village she learnt to fold the Turbant; here she was bathed and anointed . . . Lastly I shall hear how the very first Night you lay in Pera, you had a vision of Mahomet's Paradise, and happily awaked without a Soul. From that blessed instant the beautiful Body was at full liberty to perform all the agreeable functions it was made for.[69]

This Eastern Land of Cutt Cucumbers was depicted in such exaggerated manner that it was protected against the charge of taking itself seriously. Oliver Goldsmith, for example, continuing in the Oriental strain popular in the epistolary travelogues of the late eighteenth century, produced the following satire:

> I am told they have no balls, drums nor operas in the East, but then they have got a seraglio . . . Besides, I am told, your Asiatic beauties are the most convenient women alive, for they have no souls; positively there is nothing in nature I should like so much as ladies without souls; soul, here, is the utter ruin of half the sex.[70]

William Beckford's Oriental tale, *Vathek*,[71] was a precursor of the kind of Oriental narrative that the nineteenth-century Decadents would produce. It portrayed a dark, sinister and macabre Orient, with a doomed yet seductive hero reminiscent of Milton's Lucifer (the *héro maudit* who would appeal so strongly to Baudelaire). Beckford's imagination was incited by the *Arabian Nights* which had impassioned him since childhood, as well as by Orientalist texts such as d'Herbelot's *Bibliothèque Orientale* (1697), Sale's translation of the Qur'an which appeared in 1734 and included the influential 'Preliminary Discourse', and Richardson's *Dissertation on the Languages, Literature, and Manners of Eastern Nations* (1777).[72] Beckford's adulterous relationship with his cousin's wife Louisa is recreated as the relationship of Vathek and Nouronihar. The story of the over-indulged and vastly wealthy young Caliph disregarding all moral restraints in the pursuit of his appetites is, as one biographer has argued, the story of Beckford himself.[73]

The trope of the Orient as an erotic space served Beckford's creative purposes. *Vathek* came out of the eighteenth-century tradition of the oriental tale,[74] which borrowed the Orient to use as literary framework, borrowing its rich interiors and adopting its supposedly inflated linguistic styles, its *bons mots* for moralising purposes, for satiric or romantic ones. It provided an extension, a foil, a 'poetic policy' as Byron phrased it. It made use of a fictionalised East to fictionalise it further. Beckford had written to Mrs Hervey of his attraction to the Orient, but had cautioned:

> Don't fancy, my Dear Sister, I am enraptured with the orientals

themselves. It is the country they inhabit which claims all the admiration I bestow on that quarter of the Globe. It is their woods of Spice trees, their strange animals, their vast rivers which I delight in.[75]

It was this escapist *lieu* of a literary Orient that attracted him. 'My imagination roams to other countries,' he wrote, 'in search of pleasure it no longer finds at home.'[76] He was susceptible to this particular Orient as the 'most sublime form of the Romantic' (as Schlegel was), as a counteracting influence to the restraint of his native North:

> English phlegm and frostiness nips my slight texture to death. I cannot endure the composed indifference of my Countrymen. What possessed me to return amongst them? The island is lovely without doubt – its woods and verdure unparalleled. But such inhabitants! Ye Gods![77]

Later in his life, becoming more antisocial and more prone to the intense depressions that had always plagued him, Beckford withdrew to Fonthill (the architectural 'folly' where he had once celebrated his coming of age with extravagances he had borrowed from the *Arabian Nights*[78]), to the evocative atmosphere of its Egyptian Hall, where he continued his readings of Orientalist literature. Describing such evenings, he wrote:

> Mr Henley and I have toiled like Dromedaries in the Library, which I can assure you is not a little improved. Don Quixotte blazes forth in all the pomp of Morocco and golden daggers . . . The Gallery looks very solitary now poor Louisa is away. You cannot imagine the solemn appearance of the Hall with its expiring Lamps towards midnight. I often fancy myself in the Catacombs of Egypt and expect to stumble over a Mummy.[79]

Beckford's oriental tale affected the writing of two of his younger contemporaries. Both Byron and Moore owed a great deal to its construction, and benefited from the vogue that it inspired. Byron's own extravagant nature was attracted to the story's excesses, and on setting out for Greece in 1823, he retained a copy of *Vathek* but instructed that his other books be sold.[80] He made numerous efforts to meet Beckford, but that latter had been disobliging, and had written:

Oh! to what good could it possibly have led? We should have met in full drill – both talked at the same time – both endeavoured to have been delighted – a correspondence would have been established, the most insufferable and laborious that can be imagined, because the most artificial. Oh gracious goodness, I have had the opportunity of enjoying the best qualities of his mind in his works; what more do I require?[81]

Yet as J. W. Oliver has pointed out, Beckford must have avoided meeting the poet for a more profound reason; Byron was too similar to the passionate and prodigious young man he himself had been. An encounter with him was bound to be an alarming experience for one who wished to obliterate his past as completely as Beckford did.

Like Beckford, Byron was an avid reader of travel literature and of Orientalist accounts.[82] Writing to his friend Thomas Moore in 1813, he advised him to read Castellan's *Moeurs, usages, costumes des Othomans* (1812) since he thought it would provide him with the necessary meat for an Oriental poem. Byron encouraged Moore to write such a poem precisely because he thought it would be received favourably in the literary climate of the time:

Stick to the East; the oracle, Staël, told me it was the only poetic policy. The North, South, and West, have all been exhausted; but from the East, we have nothing but Southey's unsaleables . . . The little I have done in that way is merely a 'voice in the wilderness' for you; and, if it has had any success, that also will prove that the public are orientalizing, and pave the path for you.[83]

Byron advised intelligently, for Moore soon made his fortune with his Oriental metrical Romance, *Lalla Rookh* (1817), which Longman had commissioned, and for which they paid the extravagant sum of three thousand guineas. It contained a heavy dose of overblown lyrical description, such as that of beautiful scenery along the road that Lalla Rookh traverses on her way to meet her bridegroom. This particular description was criticised by the traveller Victor Jacquemont, who was no doubt irked by the tremendous popularity of such saccharine stuff: 'Thomas Moore is not only a perfumer', he grumbled, 'but a liar to boot. I am now pursuing the same route that Lalla Rookh formerly did;

and I have scarcely seen a tree since I left Delhi.'[84] Moore's
Romance contained the stock details of what the East was
supposedly like: doe-eyed women in abundance, languishing with
love and expiring of desire, wicked men who kept them in
captivity, rich banquets, gorgeous brocades and cashmeres,
jewels, perfumes, music, dance, and poetry. But this lyrical
rhapsody was not free from the traditional Western hostility to
Islam. Moore did not at all distinguish between history and
legend; there reappear in his text medieval motifs of Muhammad
as imposter, magician and sensualist, and as Moore puts into the
mouth of a Persian fire-worshipper,

> A wretch who shrines his lust in heav'n,
> And makes a pander of his God.[85]

In his *Twopenny Post Bag* (1813), in the epistle entitled 'From
Abdallah, in London, to Mohassan, in Ispahan', Moore had
quipped:

> A Persian's Heav'n is easily made,
> 'Tis but black eyes and lemonade.[86]

One of the early uses of the word 'romantic' was the seventeenth-
century's usage, 'like the old romances'.[87] Moore's *Lalla Rookh*
was romantic in that particular sense; very much like the old
medieval romances, it documented the same Orient of the
disordered imagination.

Byron was instrumental in encouraging the publication of
another poem with Oriental strains, Coleridge's *Kubla Khan*
(which was written in 1797, and published in 1816 by John
Murray, at Byron's bidding). Like Byron, Coleridge was addicted
to books of travel, especially those depicting voyages to the East.
J. B. Beer has pointed out that this literary interest served as a
poetical manoeuvre on Coleridge's part, a method of obtaining
mythological richness from the accounts perused, and a host of
startling images as well.[88] Coleridge cherished in particular
Purchas His Pilgrims (1625), Maundrell's *A Journey from Aleppo to
Jerusalem, 1697* (1707), and Bruce's *Travels to Discover the Source of the
Nile* (1790); the first two works were instrumental in the writing of
Kubla Khan – Purchas provided Coleridge with the history of
Kublai and his pleasure dome (indeed, he had been reading this

section before he 'dreamt' the poem), and Maundrell's account of
Damascus and the river 'Barrady' (Barada), as Beer has argued,[89]
furnished the imagery for the magical Xanadu of the poem.
Although Coleridge did borrow images from these travelogues,
the use he made of them fulfilled certain psychological factors in
his own make-up; 'it is evident from the unmistakably sexual
character of this imagery (dome of pleasure, caverns, fountain,
milk) that Purchas's description of a house of pleasure tapped a
reservoir of private feelings and associations'.[90] The enigmatic
details of Xanadu were apt reflections of an agitated journey
inwards. Coleridge's Orient – like Beckford's – was unsettling and
restful at once. It was a place of startling contradictions (sun and
ice, desire and satiety, beauty and grotesqueness). He entered into
it as though it were an opiate trance protecting him from vexatious
reality. In a letter of 1797 he wrote:

> I should much wish, like the Indian Vishna, to float about along
> an infinite ocean cradled in the flower of the Lotos, & wake once
> in a million years for a few minutes – just to know that I was
> going to sleep a million years more. I have put this in the mouth
> of Alhadra my Moorish woman.[91]

Coleridge had loved the *Arabian Nights* as a child; in a letter of
9 October 1797, he wrote to Thomas Poole of the 'anxious and
fearful eagerness with which I used to watch the window in which
the books lay, and whenever the sun lay upon them I would seize it
[the *Arabian Nights*], carry it by the wall, and bask and read'.[92] He
also mentioned his father's stern disapproval of the stories, how he
thought they should be burned since they impassioned children.[93]
The elder Coleridge's belief was not without foundation, for his
writings would always bear the mark of those impassioning tales.
    From the imagination's Orient, Coleridge drew his muses. His
Abyssinian maid is the spouse of poetic fancy; like Southey's
'snowy Ethiop', she is exotic but familiar – being fair-skinned like
the Circassians of Orientalist painting. She is a later version of the
Circassian Lewti in the poem of that name, in which Coleridge
adopts the trappings of traditional Persian poetry:

> I know the place where Lewti lies,
> When silent night has closed her eyes:
>   It is a breezy jasmine-bower,

The nightingale sings o'er her head:
  Voice of the Night! had I the power
That leafy labyrinth to thread,
And creep, like thee, with soundless tread,
I then might view her bosom white
Heaving lovely to my sight,
And these two swans together heave
On the gently-swelling wave.

This Coleridgian use of the East as a metaphor for sensuality and seductive sonority changed, later in the nineteenth century, into an explicit sexual message. The *Arabian Nights* was manipulated into an occasion for a sexual discourse, and the tales became valuable as text to be annotated and augmented. From being the *belle dame* of Galland's *salon*, Scheherazade changed into the gay woman of Burton's club, for private subscribers only. The Orient of the Western imagination provided respite from Victorian sexual repressiveness. It was used to express for the age the erotic longings that would have otherwise remained suppressed.

2   The Text as Pretext

In 1797, expressing doubts about the accuracy of the translation of the *Arabian Nights* that Europe was familiar with, Richard Hole wrote:

> We are of course as much acquainted with the merits of the original as we should be in respect to the former beauty of a human body from contemplating its skeleton.[1]

He was thus expressing, albeit prematurely, a preoccupation with the textual accuracy of the *Arabian Nights* that was to prevail in the nineteenth century. This was one manifestation of the quest for the historical origins of the tales. They appealed to the intellect seeking cultural data, and they became important as sociological document as well as diverting narrative. In the preface to his translation of the *Arabian Nights*, Henry Torrens delineated his intention as 'less to give the incident of a tale, than the manners of a people',[2] This intention was to find its culmination with E. W. Lane's translation, where the text is mainly a pretext for a long sociological discourse on the East. Lane's translation deliberately relegated the romantic machinery to a secondary place. An article in the *Athenaeum* (25 September 1841), published a year after Lane's translation appeared, commended such a shift in emphasis claiming that the vogue for romance was on the wane since it was at 'variance with the spirit of the age'. 'The nineteenth century', the article continued, 'is distinguished by a craving for the positive and the real – it is essentially an age of analysis and criticism.' Lane's version of the *Arabian Nights* catered to such a craving for the real. He had made a self-conscious effort to place the stories in an historical and sociological framework by appending extensive notes to them. He considered the stories' value to lie in the 'fullness and fidelity with which they describe the character, manners and customs of the Arabs'.[3]

Lane had already earned a reputation as a describer of such

things; his work, *Manners and Customs of the Modern Egyptians* (1836), had come to be considered (by the time he published his translation of *The Thousand and One Nights* in 1841) the definitive text on how Muslims lived and behaved. This work had developed from Lane's notes for a section intended to form part of a comprehensive work on both ancient and modern Egypt (of which there only remains a draft[4]). However, Lane's initial plan was altered considerably when he was offered a subsidy by the Society for the Diffusion of Useful Knowledge to produce a book on modern Egypt for a series entitled 'The Library of Entertaining Knowledge'. He returned to Egypt in 1834 in order to augment his notes, and set up temporary household there. He wrote in the Introduction to *Modern Egyptians*:

> What I have principally aimed at, in this work, is correctness; and I do not scruple to assert that I am not conscious of having endeavoured to render interesting any matter that I have related by the slightest sacrifice of truth.[5]

Such an overburdened and cautious sentence implied how acutely aware Lane was of the wiles used traditionally by travellers to 'render interesting' the matters they related. He no doubt strove, as a self-appointed expert on the Orient, to avoid the blatant exaggerations of less erudite narrators. Yet Lane could not help falling victim to the common distortion of selectivity – of choosing to stress mainly what would interest a Western reader. Thus he wrote a great deal about magic, astrology and alchemy, about hemp and opium, serpent-charmers and public dancers, enumerating superstitions and recounting bizarre incidents of a sensational nature. His tone, however, remained deceptively dry in sharp contrast to the kind of material he was describing. This gave his writing a semblance of scholarship and encouraged in his readers a total suspension of disbelief.

One of Lane's most conspicuous preoccupations was the need to appear truthful. He wished to present his evidence in a way that would ensure it full credence. Therefore, when he recounted an incident that he himself had not witnessed directly, he assured his audience that he had been informed of its details by a very reliable source. For instance, when speaking of the feats performed by Egyptian magicians, he says: 'I have stated these facts partly from my own experience, and partly as they came to my knowledge on the authority of respectable persons.'[6] These respectable persons, Lane soon reveals, are fellow Englishmen. Their authority cannot be suspect, for they are guarded against the possibility of dubious testimony by the strength of their nationality. Lane's enthusiasm for magical practices had been awakened in the first instance by a compatriot, as this passage elucidates: 'A few days after my arrival in this country, my curiosity was excited on the subject of magic by a circumstance related to me by Mr Salt, our Consul-general.'[7] Europeans in the East depended on each other's testimony to sustain their communal image of the Orient. Lane's book became a classic mainly because it instructed England about Egypt in keeping with a long tradition, using a system of thought that remained untainted by the very location it was describing. James Aldridge, for example, continuing to rely on the 'incestuousness' of European testimony, admired Lane's book as a revelation and described it as 'the most truthful and detailed account in English of how Egyptians lived and behaved'.[8] Indeed the very fact that the book was in English *made* it 'the most truthful and detailed account' – its Englishness was not merely a linguistic coincidence; rather, it conveyed cultural and political status. Lane's account was a vital contribution to the tradition of conceptualising the Orient, turning it into assimilable information. The Society that assisted him financially in his endeavour did so precisely because he fulfilled its aspirations: he was, aptly enough for its purposes, a diffuser of 'Useful Knowledge'. He offered his society a capacious picture of Egypt; Egypt, that is, for Western consumption and coloured by Western bias.

Lane upheld many of the traditional Western epithets about the Easterner in his narrative. He considered the native to be indolent, superstitious, sensually over-indulgent and religiously fanatical. The narrative structure built around these views was constructed in a manner that could be highly deceptive. It professed itself to be unemotional and unerring, highly-specialised yet all-encompassing. It seemed to be non-fictional, descriptive rather than evaluative, enumerative in technique and apparently scholastic.

Examined more closely, this narrative whose author had subtly set himself up as the central hero and the main authority was fictionalising the world it was describing. It fashioned a scene where certain details were augmented, and others carefully omitted. The dry tone in which Lane wrote furthered the illusion of scholarship and demarcated the boundaries of English interaction with the East. Reticent prudery marked many of the anecdotes that Lane offered his readers; often, when describing a mode of behaviour he wished to imply existed in the East – and only there – he would interrupt his own account as being too risqué for an erudite European to write, or a respectable European to read. This sort of interruption, though couched in terms of conscientious morality, served mainly to add to the titillating nature of the narrative; the East was full of strange apparitions, and some were too erotic or too violent even to be evoked in language. Thus the image of the mute seraglio, with its hidden dangers and pleasures, the bulk of its details for ever unarticulated, reappears before the reader. This partially-revealed location is implicit in the following description of hired dancing-girls:

> Some of them, when they exhibit before a private party of men, wear nothing but the shintiyan (or trousers) and a tob (or very full, long, wide-sleeved shirt or gown) of semi-transparent, coloured gauze, open nearly half-way down the front . . . The scenes which ensue cannot be described.[9]

When writing of magicians' tricks, a subject that fascinated Lane especially since magic and sorcery were traditionally linked in the European imagination with the Orient, he begins to describe one trick, interrupting himself at the crucial point:

> 'Several indecent tricks which he performs with the boy I must abstain from describing: some of them are abominably disgusting.'[10]

In his Introduction, after stating that he aspires to correctness, Lane introduces his readers to the first 'Modern Egyptian', the Sheikh Ahmad. This man had two unfortunate characteristics: a liking for polygamy, and a strong penchant for eating glass. Indeed, his appetite seemed to have been so strong that he managed to consume one of Lane's chandeliers. The reader makes his acquaintance with this proffered Orient through this bizarre personage (who, Lane coyly states, is not particularly representative of the whole Egyptian nation), only to be led on through a still more fantastic labyrinth of characters and incidents.

Lane chose singular images of depravity in order to make the East into a 'living tableau of queerness'[11] – to the sheikh who ate glass he added the 'saint' who cut himself open and displayed his intestines for the public's entertainment during a marriage ceremony. Also conspicuous is the following unsavoury image which encapsulates within itself the Orient of a hostile imagination:

> Some women step over the body of a decapitated man seven times, without speaking, to become pregnant; and some, with the same desire, dip in the blood a piece of cotton wool, of which they afterwards make use in a manner I must decline mentioning.[12]

In associating the Orient with a perverted sexuality, Lane was merely reiterating a tenacious Western bias. He stressed the promiscuity of Egyptian women, and their uncontrollable licentiousness.[13]

Lane's generalisations about the Egyptian character continue with a predictability that verges on the comical. The Egyptians are sexually inflammable, and easily excited to quarrel.[14] They are obstinate and remarkable for their cupidity. They are, Lane testifies (falling back on a strong tradition of portraying the native as a liar and a cheat) incapable of telling the truth: 'Constant veracity', he says, 'is a virtue extremely rare in modern Egypt'.[15]

Everything held in awe by the Egyptian populace Lane dispassionately ridicules. 'The Arabs are a very superstitious people; and none of them are more so than those of Egypt.'[16] Lane pontificates on some of their religious beliefs in a manner that is reminiscent of earlier and cruder polemic against Islam: 'Most of the reputed saints of Egypt', he writes, 'are either lunatics, or idiots, or imposters.'[17] This sentence in particular has a parallel in Joseph Pitts's popular account of his 'abduction' by Muslims and his period as a slave amongst them. In one passage he relates:

> They have a great Veneration for idiots, accounting them no less than inspired; and the reason is, because Mahomet, when he devoted himself to a solitary life in the Cave near Mecca, by

much Fasting, and an austere Way of living, greatly impair'd
his Health, so that he began to talk, and behave himself like a
natural.[18]

After addressing himself to a description of Egyptian ignorance
('Of geography, the Egyptians in general,' he says, 'have scarcely
any knowledge'), Lane offers an apologia for the nation's
shortcomings:

> Such being the state of science among the modern Egyptians,
> the reader will not be surprised at finding the present chapter
> on science followed by a long account of their superstitions; a
> knowledge of which is necessary to enable him to understand
> their character, and to make due allowance for many of its
> faults.[19]

This nation, with the character of its inhabitants so heavily
plagued by faults, had only one hope for improvement: the
enlightenment that could be brought it through contact with the
West:

> We may hope for, and, indeed, reasonably expect, a very great
> improvement in the intellectual and moral state of this people,
> in consequence of the introduction of European sciences, by
> which Mohammad 'Alee, in some degree, made amends for his
> oppressive sway.[20]

Lane's optimism, however, is shortlived. The Egyptians are too
far gone in ignorance to show the benefits in their moral and
intellectual faculties of Western education. Lane therefore refutes
his own expectations of Egyptian enlightenment, saying that 'it is
not probable that this hope will soon be realised to any
considerable extent'.[21]

Although *Modern Egyptians* was but a single manifestation of an
impressively prolific Orientalist career, it did reflect Lane's beliefs
more concisely than any of his other works.[22] It offered the
authoritative resumé of what a gentleman-scholar believed the
East to be like. It enshrined his experience, and it did so without
seeming at all subjective. Lane's Modern Egypt, although
described with less crudity and with more insight, did
nevertheless share a great deal with Lord Cromer's vision in his

Modern Egypt. Thus the scholar and the imperialist tended to voice similar sentiments, perceive their surroundings in concordant ways, and struggle under the same white man's burden. They were custodians of the heritage of Orientalism, and they could not escape its traps, even had they wished to. Lane's patronising tone foreshadowed that of Cromer, who wrote:

> Let us, in Christian charity, make every possible allowance for the moral and intellectual shortcomings of the Egyptians, and do whatever can be done to rectify them.[23]

But Cromer's Christian charity, like Lane's academic optimism, did not run very deep. It was very difficult to see beyond imperialism and imagine independent colonies:

> It may be that at some future period the Egyptians may be rendered capable of governing themselves without the presence of a foreign army in their midst and without foreign guidance in civil and military affairs, but that period is far distant.[24]

Lane's translations of the *Arabian Nights*, the main text that Europe continued to borrow from Arabic and transfer into its own literatures, confirmed the portrayal of a decadent East. Lane's version, however, in the nineteenth-century manner, presented this same myth under a more subtle guise – that of scholarship. Lane attached to his text the paraphernalia of academic discourse: he introduced, footnoted, expanded upon and augmented a frivolous text, making it seem thus an important and culturally reflective one. Lane's notes were closely related to the text (unlike Burton's, who digressed for his own purposes, as we shall see), clinging to a particular image in it and defining it, anchoring it to a larger panorama of Eastern life. For example, when a messenger leaves Shahzaman's court bearing a letter to the king's brother, Lane pauses for a definition of the 'letters of Muslims', acquainting his reader with the fact that the paper used is thick, and white, and sometimes ornamented with flowers – 'the upper half is generally left blank: the writing never occupies any portion of the second side . . . The name of the person to whom the letter is addressed commonly occurs in the first sentence, preceded by several titles of honour'[25] – and continues in this droning tone to list what seem to him important peculiarities of letter-presentation. When a character in one of the tales enters a salon, Lane meditates on Arab furnishings and reflects on architectural styles. In onè particularly unlikely place for such deliberation, in the tale of 'The Porter and The Three Ladies of Baghdad', Lane informs his readers in a footnote that windows 'commonly project outwards, and are furnished with mattresses and cushions'. Rising to a description of ceilings, he continues: 'The ceiling is of wood, and certain portions of it, which are carved, or otherwise ornamented by fanciful carpentry, are usually painted with bright colours, such as red, green, and blue, and sometimes varied with gilding.'[26] When the princess of the Ebony Island offers sherbet to a guest, Lane establishes that 'sherbet is served in covered glass cups', and that these 'are placed on a round tray, and covered with a round piece of embroidered silk, or cloth of gold'.[27] Lane's notes appear more and more oppressive as one reads on; no arbitrary detail is left hermetic – each is pinned down like an ill-fated butterfly by Lane's imperturbable attestations. Repeatedly, the course of the light-hearted narrative is stayed to accommodate Lane's parallel and dictatorial narrative; the text for him is pretext, the translation a mere vessel for his counterpart deliberations. When a genie is mentioned in a tale, Lane recounts in detail Muslim beliefs and conceptions of genii[28]; when a genie's son dies, Lane defines Muslim conceptions of fate, the afterworld, as he had described the tenets of Islam, the 'Arabian System of Cosmography', and the laws governing society.

Lane's intention in this translation was the same as his intention in *Modern Egyptians*: to present the Orient as fully as possible, to contain it in narrative, to comprehend its elements and to fit them into an amenable structure. Lane's purpose was to deliver Egypt and the Egyptians to his readers, 'to keep nothing hidden, to deliver the Egyptians without depth, in swollen detail'.[29] Lane wished to achieve the 'imposition of a scholarly will upon an untidy reality',[30] to appear only in the reserved persona of annotator and translator and lexicographer.[31] The humanity of Lane's narrative undertaking was sacrificed – intentionally sacrificed, for Lane was a highly self-conscious craftsman – in favour of scientific validity. He was the Empire's scholar, surveying its dominions, portraying its subjects, recounting their culture in the unemotive and urbane manner that he assumed befitted his status.

One revealing episode in Lane's life took place in 1831, when his friend Robert Hay offered him a female slave named Nefeeseh he had bought. This triggered a classic series of reactions: Lane installed her as his servant, attempted to prod her into reducing her fat, undertook the task of educating her ('she is making satisfactory progress in reading and writing, as well as needlework; which, with arithmetic, are all the accomplishments I wish her to acquire'[32]), and ultimately, after much confusion of feeling varying from contempt to dependence, made her his wife. Lane's relationship with Nefeeseh paralleled his relation with the Orient in general; he was the mentor and the figure of power, and they were bound to him in tutelage.

Lane's narrative (both in *Modern Egyptians* and in his translation of the *Arabian Nights*) was highly genteel, conforming to the ethical codes of middle-class morality. It strove to inform without offending, to place before the Victorian public an East tailor-fitted to please. Lane made a deliberate effort to weed out seemingly objectionable incidents or descriptions, all that might have offended an increasingly squeamish middle-class readership.[33] His intention was to produce a useful, enlightening and sober family book, but one that would nevertheless bear the imprint of his learning. His prudery ended by complementing Burton's pruriency: each man used the *Arabian Nights* to express his personality and his preoccupations, and both of their texts taken together illustrated the contradictory penchants of the Victorian age.

BURTON: SOLDIER AND SCRIBE

When Richard Burton was eight, leading a mobile life on the Continent with his family, his mother stood him and his younger brother Edward outside a pastry-shop window, and, pointing to some apple puffs in the display, proceeded to lecture her sons on the virtues of self-denial. This proved to be too much for her wild first-born, who smashed the glass before them, clawed out the cakes, and left his mother in the embarrassing position of paying for the damages as he bolted down the street to enjoy himself.

This apocryphal anecdote points to a personality trait that would never leave Burton; a wilfulness that bid him defy every authority, and a consistent urge to break any imposed rule in as startling a manner as possible. His defiance of parental authority changed, when he was sent to Oxford against his wishes, into a defiance of academic tutors. He rebelled constantly during his brief stay at the University, and would neither conform to social decorum nor mask his contempt for the set curriculum. He later recounted how he had made that contempt obvious to his superiors. When trying for a fellowship in Classics, he chose to pronounce Greek as it was pronounced by the Modern Greeks, and not in the manner he knew was favoured at Oxford. This annoyed his examiners, and the award went to a more complacent (if less linguistically-gifted) candidate. This was to be the first, but by no means the last, of the setbacks that Burton's career would suffer due to his inability to meet the niceties of social intercourse.

It was out of this urge to be contrary and different that Burton's desire to learn Arabic originally sprang. There were, at that time in Oxford, no proper arrangements for Arabic tuition. Burton was determined to raise a fuss until a tutor be found him. He then embarked upon what would be a life-long journey into the labyrinth of that language. It was, at least in Oxford, a labyrinth entirely to himself; no one cared to compete in its exploration, and thus no one threatened the peace of its edgy devotee.

However, the confines of Oxford soon proved too taxing for one of Burton's disposition. He made himself unruly enough to be sent down, and exited noisily on a tandem, crushing, along with some prized flower-beds, all hopes of an academic career.

It was for India and the army that he headed. For if he felt uneasy in parochial Oxford, he felt quite at ease in the larger context of British colonial society on the sub-continent. In an examination of some traits of Burton's personality, Kathryn Tidrick remarks this colonial identification:

> He came to identify himself less with England, Shakespeare's sceptr'd isle, than with Greater Britain, the Empire. He would never have professed a patriotism like Wilfrid Blunt's, founded on love of the ancestral soil; Burton's patriotism had to express itself imperially, because only in the imperial enterprise was there a place for misfits like him.[34]

For the young Burton fresh from academic disaster and family chastisement, India proved a much needed haven. It was the gateway through which he could pass into adulthood, into experiences more varied than those he could have expected in England. It was a novelty to become acquainted with new languages, a new population, new ways of thought. It appealed to many of Burton's whims – his urge to court danger, his sexual curiosity, his linguistic insatiability, and his hankering after power and delight in disguise. Recalling that first arrival in India, he wrote of how he had devised means of ingratiating himself into the new environment, a difficult process needing the exercise of all his talents:

> The first difficulty was to pass for an Oriental, and this was as necessary as it was difficult. The European official in India seldom, if ever, sees anything in its real light, so dense is the veil which the fearfulness, the duplicity, the prejudice, and the superstitions of the natives hang before his eyes.[35]

Wishing to peer beyond that veil of native duplicity, as he saw it, Burton felt the need to disguise his real identity. He became (on staining his skin with walnut juice and donning local garb) the 'European official' as well as the native, aptly illustrating in that duality the nature of the white man's presence in the East. For there were two sides to the British gentleman in those remote parts: the Empire man who was authoritative by inclination as well as by position, and his *Doppelgänger*, the rebel who longed to escape from authority of all kind. He craved a freedom he could not have been allowed at home (and as such, was the forerunner of the modern hippy).

One aspect of this desired freedom was sexual. Burton's first complete sexual initiation took place in India. Like many of his peers, he sought the services of a local woman who (as generally accepted in the barracks of British India) would cater to his physical needs without expecting any moral or emotional commitment. She was the *bubu* (the coloured sister, as Burton refers to her) who kept house and was the sexual outlet. Burton, who pondered these matters a great deal more than most of his compatriots, noticed that although the woman was compliant and seemingly complacent, she hardly ever felt 'love' for her keeper:

> while thousands of Europeans have cohabited for years with and have had families by native women, they are never loved by them – at least I have never heard of a single case.[36]

Burton attributed this lack of romantic attachment on the part of
the native woman to the European's clumsy sexual techniques.
The Westerner could not meet the demands imposed upon him by
the native woman's body (who could not be satisfied, as Burton
had calculated, with less than twenty minutes[37]), and could
therefore never win her affections. Perhaps it never occurred to
Burton, at ease within the patriarchal values of the colonial
enterprise, that the native woman might not have felt attachment
for the European for different – and more complex – reasons than
those he chose as explanation. The European, after all, had
occupied her land, oppressed her people, and imposed his
personal will upon her. Her emotional detachment was her only
defence – feeble as it was – against total victimisation. He had the
power to enslave her, but he could not *make* her love him.

Burton's ideas about Eastern women never gained in depth
even after he had spent decades in the East. They would always be
patterned on the master-slave relationship he had become
habituated to in India. The woman was chattel and sexual
convenience; as such, she was necessary, but she could never
attain the stature of true spouse. Although an anarchist in his
superficial social behaviour, Burton always retained his age's
polarised view of women. They were either sexual beings who
were whorish, or caring companions in the home, untinged by
sexual ardour. Burton's fascination with the *Arabian Nights* was
greatly enhanced by the fact that they upheld his own views on
women, race and class.

The tales of the *Arabian Nights* were originally recounted to an
all male audience desiring bawdy entertainment. They were
purposefully crude, and pandered to the prejudices of the
uneducated men who listened to them being narrated. They
provided wish-fulfilling descriptions of endless riches to a humble
listener. They reaffirmed particular xenophobic biases and
denigrated local minorities. But above all, they reflected a certain
mode of apprehending women prevalent in the repressively
patriarchal societies of which they were the product.

The depictions of women in the *Arabian Nights* can be arranged
in two classic categories. The first category is by far the larger one,
containing the negative stereotypes who embody all the vices
traditionally associated with the female (associations that crop up
in almost every culture) and ones which are supposedly peculiar
to her. The women are demonesses, procuresses, sorceresses,

witches. They are fickle, faithless and lewd. They are irrepressively malign, and plot to achieve their base desires in the most merciless manner imaginable. Indeed, the tales begin with numerous examples of wanton women. The frame-tale sets the tone for the rest of the stories: Shahzaman's queen befouls his bed (as soon as his back is turned) with one of his black slaves. Before he has time to digest this shock, he discovers his brother's queen dallying in the exact same manner with another black slave during *her* husband's absence. Having wrought their revenge respectively on their unfaithful spouses, the two kings embark on a journey together only to be accosted by a lascivious dame who bids them tup her in turn. Having achieved her desire of them (and having added their signet rings to her large collection taken from men she has abducted), she commences to recount to them her history, how she has consistently managed to outwit the jealous *ifrit* whose captive she is:

> Of a truth this Ifrit bore me off on my bridenight, and put me in a casket in a coffin and to the coffin he affixed seven strong padlocks of steel and deposited me on the deep bottom of the sea that raves, dashing and clashing with waves; and guarded me so that I might remain chaste and honest, quotha! that none save himself might have connexion with me. But I have lain under as many of my kind as I please, and this wretched Jinni wotteth not that Destiny may not be averted nor hindered by aught, and that whatso woman willeth the same she fulfilleth however man nilleth.[38]

Assured of womens' inherent lechery and treachery from the horse's mouth, as it were, the two kings decide to return to their kingdoms, with Shahrayar vowing to take his revenge on womanhood by taking a virgin to wife every night and having her beheaded in the morning.

The tales abound with descriptions of lecherous women who copulate with anyone, anywhere. In the 'Tale of the Ensorcelled Prince', the prince's wife leaves her husband's bed every night (after having him drugged with a sleeping-potion) in order to go to a hovel on the other side of the city and lie with a leprous black. He abuses her with various obscene epithets, makes her eat rat-stew, and rages at her for being late: when she tries to defend herself, he becomes angrier, and shouts:

Thou liest, damn thee! Now I swear an oath by the valour and
honour of blackamoor men (and deem not our manliness to be
the poor manliness of white men), from today forth if thou stay
away till this hour, I will not keep company with thee nor will I
glue my body with thy body and strum and belly-bump. Dost
thou play fast and loose with us, thou cracked pot, that we may
satisfy thy dirty lusts? stinkard! bitch! vilest of the vile whites![39]

The woman is not at all offended by such abuse, and continues to
abase herself before her lover until he agrees to lie with her. Her
lust once satisfied, she makes her way back to her husband's
palace.

Women of this type are portrayed as being gratuitously cruel.
They take pleasure from inflicting pain, and they devise all
manner of outlandish torture. The heroine of the 'Reeve's Tale',
for instance, becomes so offended when her lover comes to her still
smelling of 'cumin-ragout' that she reacts in the following
manner:

'I will teach thee how to eat cumin-ragout without washing thy
hands!' Then she cried to her handmaids, who pinioned me;
and she took a sharp razor and cut off my thumbs and great
toes.[40]

The second category of women in the *Arabian Nights* (and the less
important one) contains women who are pious and prudent. They
are usually either well-brought up virgins who fall victim to a
cruel fate before being corrupted (for all women are corruptible),
or pious wives or mothers who are not disturbingly sexual. Their
beauty poses no threat to the *status quo*. They are kind and good
and their kindness and goodness is usually a decorative foil to the
story-line, but of no great dramatic value.

Scheherazade is the only 'saving stereotype',[41] for she is
described as being both good and physically desirable, intelligent,
pious, learned and dutiful. Yet her innocent nature is in sharp
contrast to the bawdiness of her stories. Her inexperience is at
odds with the *risqué* tale she tells. She describes the crafty and
malicious wiles of women to the king in one tale after another: she
survives by condemning her kind. She sides with the king against
her own sex, and is thus allowed to keep her head. She is
exemplary in all the domestic roles; dutiful daughter, considerate

sister, loving wife and caring mother. Although she is highly learned, her learning serves only to please and placate a man – it has no other function at all. Her knowledge of the world is all from books, for she has no real experience of any kind. She has no separate existence either, for she moves from her father's house into the king's bedroom, where she remains chained to her narrative for a thousand and one nights. She is only superficially powerful; her feeble spell is piteously inconsequential, for one word from the king could defeat the whole range of her story, and take her life.

Such representations of women were in keeping with the general Victorian prejudice. All women were inferior to men; Eastern women were doubly inferior, being women *and* Easterners. They were an even more conspicuous commodity than their Western sisters. They were part of the goods of empire, the living rewards that white men could, if they wished to, reap. They were there to be used sexually, and if it could be suggested that they were inherently licentious, then they could be exploited with no qualms whatsoever. Thus the *Arabian Nights* helped perpetuate the Victorian notion of promiscuous Eastern women, and Burton's translation in particular gave added substance to the myth. His footnotes and addenda articulated for the West the 'carnal' nature of native women. In the frame-tale of the *Arabian Nights*, for example, when the queen is discovered in the arms of a black slave, Burton cannot resist offering the following bit of 'information':

> Debauched women prefer negroes on account of the size of their parts. I measured one man in Somaliland who, when quiescent, numbered nearly six inches. This is characteristic of the negro race and of African animals; e.g. the horse; whereas the pure Arab, man and beast, is below the average of Europe; one of the best proofs by the by, that the Egyptian is not an Asiatic, but a negro partially whitewashed . . . In my time, no honest Hindi Moslem would take his womenfolk to Zanzibar on account of the huge attractions and enormous temptations there and thereby offered.[42]

These debauched women, even when kept away from the 'huge attractions and enormous temptations' in Zanzibar, could not be shamed into curbing their sexual appetites. Burton recounts that frustrated Persian women burst in upon British soldiers in the hope that they would offer them sexual relief:

> During the unhappy campaign of 1856–57 in which, with the exception of a few brilliant skirmishes, we gained no glory . . . there was a formal outburst of the Harems; and even women of princely birth could not be kept out of the officers' quarters.[43]

Eastern women were not only irrepressively lecherous, but devilish as well. Burton quotes 'Oriental' wisdom, applauding its view of women as demonesses:

> Orientals are aware that the period of especial feminine devilry is between the first menstruation and twenty when, according to some, every girl is a possible murderess. So they wisely marry her and get rid of what is called the 'lump of grief', the domestic calamity – a daughter.[44]

It is interesting to compare Burton's attitude with Lane's. Although the two were strikingly different personalities, they did share the same attitudes and the same biases. Here is the sober Lane on Eastern female devilry:

> The women of Egypt have the character of being the most licentious in their feelings of all females who lay any claim to be considered as members of a civilized nation . . . What liberty they have, many of them, it is said abuse; and most of them are not considered safe unless under lock and key . . . It is believed that they possess a degree of cunning in the management of their intrigue which the most prudent and careful of husbands cannot guard against . . . some of the stories of the intrigues of women in *The Thousand and One Nights* present faithful pictures of occurrences not infrequent in the modern metropolis of Egypt.[45]

Lane believed that the behaviour of Eastern women was unique; it had no equivalent in the West at all. Even a European prostitute was not capable of the obscenity that Egyptian women indulged in: 'things are named, and subjects talked of by the most genteel women, that many prostitutes in our own country would probably abstain from mentioning'.[46]

These depraved women indulged in countless perversions of

which European women were happily unaware. In a nineteenth-century courtcase in Scotland, when a charge of lesbianism was levelled against two mistresses of a school where a Miss Cumming was boarder, the judges 'proved' that the women were innocent by declaring them incapable of committing a sin that did not exist in Britain. They dismissed the charge, indignant at Miss Cumming (who was half Indian) for having made such an accusation in the first place:

> The judges suggested that Miss Cumming, having been raised in the lascivious East, had no idea of the horror such an accusation would stir in Britain.

> Lord Meadowbank explained . . . that he had been to India, and he would venture to guess that Miss Cumming had developed her curiosity about sexual matters from her lewd Indian nurses, who were, in contrast to British women, entirely capable of obscene chatter on such subjects.

> Lord Boyle, on the other hand, did not believe tribadism impossible among savages, but certainly improbable in civilized Britain.[47]

Burton shared this same view of tribadism as being a deviation that existed as a matter of course in the East.

> The Moslem Harem is a great school for this 'Lesbian (which I call Atossan) love'; these tribades are mostly known by peculiarities of form and features, hairy cheeks and upper lips, gruff voices, hircine odour and the large projecting clitoris with erectile powers.[48]

According to Burton, the harems of Syria were active centres of 'sapphism':

> Wealthy harems, as I have said, are hot-beds of Sapphism and Tribadism. Every woman past her first youth has a girl whom she calls her 'Myrtle' (in Damascus).[49]

With this talk of Damascene Myrtles, Burton had broken the Victorian taboo of masking sexuality. Yet he managed to do so only by speaking of sexuality in a removed setting – the East. His was a language of enumeration of perversions, deviations, excesses. He took the traditional seraglio of the Western imagination and shaded in details that would give it the appearance of *vraisemblance*. He recounted such details in the pseudo-scholarly manner he so delighted in:

> In many Harems and girls' schools tallow-candles and similar succedania are vainly forbidden and bananas when detected are cut into four so as to be useless; of late years, however, China has sent some marvellous artificial phalli of stuffed bladder, horn and even caoutchouc, the latter material of course borrowed from Europe.[50]

If the East 'borrowed from Europe' caoutchouc to fashion dildoes out of it, it was because that East, in Burton's mind, was preoccupied with sexuality, with animal existence, with languor. Pope's Land of Cutt Cucumbers reappears in Burton's narrative, but without the self-mocking tone of the former, with the heavier self-satisfaction of nineteenth-century discourse. Burton sums up the Arab's *kayf* (a word he thought untranslatable into English, presumably because he thought no equivalent state could exist in the West), seeing in it Eastern eroticism at its fullest:

> And this is the Arab's Kayf. The savouring of animal existence; the passive enjoyment of mere sense; the pleasant languor, the dreamy tranquillity, the airy castle-building, which in Asia stand in lieu of the vigorous, intensive, passionate life of Europe. It is the result of a lively, impressible excitable nature, and exquisite sensibility of nerve; it argues a voluptuousness unknown to northern regions, where happiness is placed in the exertion of mental and physical powers.[51]

Thus the East, unlike Europe where men exerted themselves to produce and excel, was peopled by nations who were content to achieve in the erotic domain alone. To uphold this assertion, Burton presented such evidence as he had culled in his capacity as expert on the Orient:

> The accidents of my life, it may be said without undue presumption, my long dealings with Arabs and other Mohammedans, and my familiarity not only with their idiom

but with their turn of thought, and with that racial individuality that baffles description, have given me certain advantages over the average student, however deeply he may have studied. These volumes, moreover, afford me a long-sought opportunity of noticing practices and customs which interest all mankind and which 'Society' will not hear mentioned . . . The student who adds the notes of Lane [*Arabian Society*, etc., before quoted] to mine will know as much of the Moslem East and more than many Europeans who have spent half their lives in Orient lands.[52]

Burton's notes, then (as well as the bulk of his writings on the East), if added to the findings of other Western witnesses, could sum up the Orient, encapsulate it into easily digestible knowledge, into assimilable fact. Yet this web of Orientalist knowledge, so studiously fashioned and so carefully wrought, could not but entangle its fashioner despite himself. Thomas Assad has suggested that Burton had, in his attempt to produce a sensual East, been himself enmeshed by it – he could no longer see and feel life except on the mere physical plane, without depth, and in chaotic detail.[53]

BURTON'S INNER CIRCLE

Burton's erotic 'translations' were privately printed and were circulated among subscribers – a leisured male audience desiring erudite titillation.

One of Burton's friends and most enthusiastic readers was Richard Monckton Milnes, who kept in his Fryston library the largest known collection of pornography in his day. Burton kept up a correspondence[54] in which he addressed Milnes as 'Carissimo', writing him without fail from Dahomey or Fernando Po, regretting his absence and anticipating their reunion.

Milnes had a greatly active interest in flagellation, and had written a poem on the subject, which Burton suggested the title 'The Birchiad'.[55] Milnes, like Burton, was fascinated by sexual deviancy, and perhaps this common taste cemented their friendship even further.

Milnes's library at Fryston had been augmented by the efforts of one Fred Hankey, who was his chief advisor and agent for the purchase of books. Hankey was in many ways the architect of the collection, which was marked by his outrageous tastes.[56] When the Goncourt brothers met him in Paris in 1862, Edmond noted in his journal:

> Aujourd'hui j'ai visité un fou, un mônstre, un de ces hommes qui confinent à l'abîme. Par lui, comme par une voile dechirée, j'ai entrevu un fonds abominable, un côté effrayant d'une aristocratie anglaise apportant la ferocité dans l'amour, et dont le libertinage ne jouit que par la souffrance de la femme.[57]

Hankey remarked to the Goncourt brothers that Paris was less amusing than London, for in London there was an establishment where one could go to whip little girls ('les petites, oh! pas très fort, mais les grandes tout à fait fort. On pouvait aussi leur enfoncer des épingles.'[58]) Hankey told them of how he had corrupted the mind of a bookbinder, who had at first refused to comply with his directions, by lending him choice books, initiating him in the sexual pursuit of little girls which led to the ruin of his marriage. Apparently, Hankey preferred to have his books bound in human skin, preferably stripped from a live female. He explained to the Goncourts how he often had trouble obtaining this article. His friend Burton, however, had promised to help him out: 'Heureusement, j'ai mon ami le docteur Bartsch, vous savez, celui qui voyage dans l'intérieur de l'Afrique. Eh bien, il m'a promis de me faire prendre une peau comme-ça . . . sur une négresse vivante.'[59] Unfortunately for him, Burton arrived in Dahomey only to find a much tamer scene than the one he and his friends had predicted. He wrote to Milnes of this letdown:

> I have been here three days and am grievously disappointed. Not a man killed, nor a fellow tortured. The canoe floating in blood is a myth of myths. Poor Hankey must still wait for his *peau de femme*.[60]

Burton asked after Hankey in almost all his letters to Milnes. He must have developed a strong empathy for him. Hankey appealed to Burton's own desire to shock and disturb; Burton had always projected an image of himself as sybarite, and had circulated the rumour of his having killed a man in Mecca, in order to pose as a Satanic figure.

Hankey's tastes, however, were pathological, and could hardly be viewed in a sympathetic light. Hankey collected instruments of torture as well as pornographic books and objects. He had once rented rooms overlooking a square where a murderess was to be hanged, and had engaged the services of prostitutes in order to take his pleasure as he watched the woman die. Milnes and Burton both found such peculiarities to their liking, and cherished him as a petted curiosity.

Another of Milnes's protégés was Charles Algernon Swinburne, the masochist in the circle to complement Hankey's sadism. Milnes had decided to take Swinburne's education in hand: with this intention, he introduced him to the writings of de Sade, and to Richard Burton. Swinburne's masochism had been immeasurably encouraged by his experiences under a practised sadist tutor at Eton. Swinburne had asked Milnes for de Sade's books, for 'the mystic pages of the martyred marquis de Sade; ever since which [you spoke of him], the vision of that illustrious and illrequited benefactor of humanity has hovered by night before my eyes'.[61] But de Sade soon proved a trifle tame for Swinburne's advanced tastes; he seemed to have found him something of a joke:

I never laughed so much in my life: I couldn't have stopped to save the said life. I went from text to illustrations and back again, till I literally doubled up and fell down with laughter – I regret to add that all the friends to whom I have lent or shown the book [*Charenton*] were affected in the same way . . . Rossetti read out the dissection of the interesting Rosalie and her infant, and the rest of that refreshing episode: and I wonder to this minute that we did not raise the house by our screams of laughter.[62]

Swinburne listened spellbound to Burton when he was introduced to him at Milnes's home in 1861. Burton was regaling the company with anecdotes from his travels; he was in his element, and he excelled himself.

When Burton discovered the writings of Vatsyayana, he wrote to Milnes of his intention of translating them. He had not yet begun reading the work when he had already decided that if he found it 'thoroughly moral [he would] hope to add some notes'.[63] He was well aware of the added sexual highlight his own notes provided an already erotic text. He strove to make them as entertaining as possible, to suit the tastes of the gentleman's club he catered to.

One subject that he returned to again and again was pederasty. As a young man in India he had been commissioned by Napier to investigate the homosexual brothels and write up what he saw. He conducted this investigation in disguise, masquerading as a half-Arab, half-Persian merchant named Mirza Abdullah of Bushire. Burton's report must have been such a startlingly explicit document because it led to the ruin of his military career in India when it was discovered in a secret file that Napier had neglected to destroy after resigning his post.

Burton's notes to the *Arabian Nights* offered his audience a wide range of information about Eastern homosexual practices. Burton's tone is authoritative and imperious: it seeks to portray a complete picture that leaves no place for doubt about the nature of the East's practices. Burton offers the insider's view of the sexual Orient, presenting his account of its perversions, recreations, institutions, larding his own narration with the attestations of other European travellers:

> Chardin tells us that the houses of male prostitution were common in Persia whilst those of women were unknown: the same is the case in the present day and the boys are prepared with extreme care by diet, baths, depilation, unguents and a host of artists in cosmetics. Le Vice is looked upon at most as a peccadillo and its mention crops up in every jestbook.[64]

Burton was fascinated by brothels, as he was fascinated by all manifestations of sexuality. He hardly ever missed an opportunity of attaching to his translation of the *Arabian Nights* some footnote that would serve to further stimulate his reader's curiosity. Sometimes the sexual image he describes becomes so exaggerated that it verges on the ludicrous, as in this passage on Chinese perversities:

> The Chinese as far as we know them in the great cities are omnivorous and omnifutuentes: they are the chosen people of debauchery and their systematic bestiality with ducks, goats, and other animals is equalled only by their pederasty. Kaemfer and Orlof Toree (*Voyage en Chine*) notice the public houses for boys and youths in China and Japan. Mirabeau

(L'Anandryne) describes the tribadism of their women in hammocks. When Pekin was plundered the Harems contained a number of balls a little larger than the old musket-ball, made of thin silver with a loose pellet of brass inside somewhat like a *grelot*: these articles were placed by the woman between the labia and an up-and-down movement on the bed gave a pleasant titillation when nothing better was to be procured. They have every artifice of luxury, aphrodisiacs, erotic perfumes and singular applications.[65]

Burton's view of the Chinese as debauched, as practitioners of bestiality, of lesbianism in hammocks (!), was only one instance of his more general contempt for non-Western peoples: Sindis, Egyptians, Persians, Turks, Arabs, all came in for their share of denigration. Burton's special loathing was reserved for Africans – whom he referred to as 'the skunks of the human race'.[66]

These responses to other peoples were an intrinsic part of the imperial world-view. To perceive the East as a sexual domain, and to perceive the East as a domain to be colonised, were complementary aspirations. This kind of narrative did not only reflect strong racial bias – it reflected a deep-seated misogyny as well. Eastern women were described as objects that promised endless congress and provoked endless contempt. This passage in Burton illustrates this reductive mode of viewing Eastern women:

A peculiarity highly prized by Egyptians; the use of the constrictor vaginae muscles, the sphincter for which Abyssinian women are famous. The 'Kabbazah' (holder), as she is called, can sit astraddle upon a man and can provoke the venereal orgasm, not by wriggling and moving but by tightening and loosing the male member with the muscles of her privities, milking as it were.[67]

As it were. For Burton, the woman was reduced to 'privities', was dissected for discourse's sake. What the narrator felt himself unable to say about European women, he could unabashedly say about Eastern ones. They were there for his articulation of sex. It was in this spirit that Victorian moralists and social scientists alike often projected onto lower-class, slave or foreign women the sexual drives that they denied the bourgeois wife.[68]

Often, Burton's tone changed from that of pseudo-scholarship to that of the well-travelled gentleman recounting to the other members of his club some salty anecdotes in an after-dinner conversation. The foreigner and his sexual habits become entertaining fodder as in this account of Persian pederasty:

> I once asked a Shirazi how penetration was possible if the patient resisted with all the force of the sphincter muscle: he smiled and said, 'Ah, we Persians know a trick to get over that; we apply a sharpened tentpeg to the crupper-bone (os coccygis) and knock till he opens.'[69]

Like Gibbon, Burton often weaves into his account phrases in French, German, Italian, Greek and Latin – the latter a language used as proof of erudition and as means of enlightened censorship. He often seeks Classical equivalents to Eastern sexual practices, as in the following passage on homosexuality:

> It begins in boyhood and many Persians account for it by paternal severity. Youths arrived at puberty find none of the facilities with which Europe supplies fornication. Onanism is to a certain extent discouraged by circumcision, and meddling with the father's slave-girls and concubines would be risking cruel punishment if not death. Hence they use each other by turns, a 'puerile practice' known as Alish-Takish, the Lat. *facere vicibus* or *mutuum facere*.[70]

Burton's footnotes to the *Arabian Nights* were often irrelevant to the text they were annotating, mere additions for the purposes of entertainment, erotic highlights of a sort. In one example, when the story-line of one tale reads: 'The Sultan rejoiced with a joy which nothing could exceed, and kissed his daughter's eyes.' The footnote that Burton adds reads:

> This is a paternal salute in the East where they are particular about the part kissed. A witty and not unusually gross Persian book, called the 'Al-Namah' because all questions begin with 'Al' (the Arab article) contains one 'Al-Wajib al-busidan?' (what best deserves bussing?) and the answer is 'kus-i-nau-pashm' (a bobadilla with a young bush).[71]

Burton used the *Arabian Nights* to express himself, to articulate his sexual preoccupations. He made it serve as an occasion for documenting all manner of sexual deviation: 'tribadism' was only one, congress with animals, sexual mutilation, castration, all these were given prolonged attention. When a eunuch is mentioned in one of the tales, Burton leaps at the opportunity to offer the following titbit:

> There are many ways of making the castrato; in some (as here) only the penis is removed, in others the testes are bruised or cut off; but in all cases the animal passion remains. Almost all these neutrals have wives with whom they practise the manifold *plaisirs de la petite oie* (masturbation, tribadism, irrumation, *tête-bêche*, *feuille de rose*, etc.), till they induce the venereal orgasm. Such was the account given me by a eunuch's wife; and I need hardly say that she, like her *confrèrie*, was to be pitied. At the critical moment she held up a pillow for her husband to bite who otherwise would have torn her cheeks or breasts.[72]

Burton's curiosity was not limited to the cataloguing of sexual inclinations, but continued into what he perceived as the more engrossing detail of sexual disease. In one passage, after addressing himself to cases of genital elephantiasis, he proceeds: 'Sarcocele and hydrocele, especially of the left testes, according to the Arabs, attack all classes, and are attributed to the relaxing climate, to unrestrained sexual indulgence, and sometimes to external injury.'[73] Such an interest in sexual disease was not unique to Burton. It was an important manifestation of the era's preoccupation with medicine. This concentration on disease was in great part reflective of sexual unease and social repressiveness. Victorian science was used to uphold such beliefs as were cherished by the Victorian establishment: it played an important role in awarding credibility to misogynist or to racist ideas. For instance, in an age that was as highly repressive of its women as that age was, it is not surprising to find that those 'scientific' theories that proved the biological inferiority of women gained great currency. While Burton was presenting his readers with accounts of sexual mutilation practised abroad, his medical compatriots were performing sexual mutilation of a similar kind at home. Clitoridictimies and ovary-removals were two operations carried out with disturbing frequency in Victorian England, in an attempt to render women 'tractable, orderly, industrious and cleanly'.[74] The medical profession supported the values of patriarchy, and sought to aid in the enforcement of the acceptable image of woman, a creature who was pious, passive and passionless, an image for which Victorian women were forced to pay very dearly.

THE SAVAGE BODY

Burton's notes to the *Arabian Nights* throw light on the evolution of Victorian anthropology, reflecting as they do many of its prime preoccupations. Burton considered himself to be an anthropologist (he was a member of the Royal Anthropological Society) and wrote in the jargon of that nascent profession.

Although anthropology eventually came to be a leveller of race and culture (with works such as *The Golden Bough* comparing different cultures in order to point out similarities between them), nineteenth-century anthropology was predominantly a system for the hierarchical classification of race. As such, it was inextricably linked to the functionings of empire. Indeed, there can be no dispute that it emerged as a distinctive discipline at the beginning of the colonial era, that it became a flourishing academic profession toward its close, and that throughout its history its efforts were chiefly devoted to a description and analysis – carried out by Europeans, for a European audience – of non-European societies dominated by the West.[75] It was the colonial cataloguing of goods; the anchoring of imperial possessions into discourse.

Although discrimination against strangers (especially dark ones) was an ancient phenomenon in the West, the ideology of race was a product of the nineteenth century. The medieval concept of 'The Great Chain of Being' was adopted as a framework for race classification. The human races were believed to have stratified in ways that precluded all egalitarian advancement in their development. The Anglo-Saxon race (according to the eminent Victorians who pondered such issues) was the most highly advanced of all; it was at the pinnacle of the human hierarchy, and was therefore the master race *par excellence*.

Early anthropologists pretended to gauge a race's development by the craniological measurements of that race's individual skulls. The shape and size of the skull was supposed to indicate something of the worth of the peoples measured. One influential upholder of this particular idea was James Cowles Prichard, whose first book, *Researches into the Physical History of Mankind* (1813), presented the racial theory of hierarchical development in scientific guise. Prichard's second and more popular book, *The Natural History of Man* (1843), drew on travellers' accounts (especially Chateaubriand's *Description de l'Égypte*) to complete its ethnological discussion of the human races. Prichard's craniological measurements of the Negro skull served to uphold his particularly violent contempt for that race: he wanted to 'prove' that the black man's brain was less advanced than the white man's, that he was caught in a state of primitiveness from which it was unlikely that he would ever emerge. Burton was greatly influenced by Prichard's ideas, no doubt because they bore strong resemblance to his own racial sentiments. He thought highly enough of *The Natural History of Man* to take it on the important expedition to Tanganyika. Like Prichard, Burton considered the Semite to be more highly advanced than the Negro, whom he considered the most inferior specimen of the human race. He jeered at the Anti-Slavery Committee's emblem of the kneeling black man, 'who, properly speaking, should have been on all fours'.[76]

Burton shared his century's belief that 'Savage Man' (a term that could incorporate all non-European peoples) was a creature of instinct, controlled by sexual passions, incapable of the refinement to which the white races had evolved. He was so distinct from them that he could well be another species altogether. The native was more like an animal; indeed, Burton often spoke of African and Arab man and beast in one breath. And like the animals he was thought to resemble, the native was supposedly distinguished from civilised whites by the automatic and irrational character of his response to environmental stimuli.[77] This automatic response was so curious that it was well worth studying: the European observer set himself up as the observer of such otherness, and recorded all the physical and mental characteristics of the animal-like native. It was in this spirit that Burton took it upon himself to measure black mens' penises or theorise about the inferiority of their brains. Indeed, there was a certain morbidness in the anthropological and medical emphasis upon the greater genital development in the Negro race. This went far in giving currency to the belief that blacks had a gargantuan sexual appetite, and by extension, a lower level of consciousness. They belonged, according to Victorian racial theoreticians, to 'the age of awakening consciousness, or nascent intelligence, a state of incipiency to moral and mental development'.[78]

It is not surprising to find, therefore, that the European, when encountering in the *Arabian Nights* tales that upheld his own racial biases, should quickly take them to heart. And since these confirming tales belonged to a foreign narrative tradition, Europe could enjoy them without offence to its outward show of rational discourse on race (the same Victorians who saw blacks as little better than animals were officially committed to the anti-slavery movement). The Victorians could appreciate the grotesque caricatures of blacks and other minorities in the stories without feeling that such gross racial effrontery was in any way the fruit of their own civilised culture.

In the same manner, the misogyny inherent in the tales fitted in with the Victorian notion of women as inferior beings. Again, Europe could happily incorporate sexist perception when it was wedded to a description of the alien – for after all, the description of inferior women in the *Arabian Nights* was concentrated on *foreign* women. These could be reduced to mere bodies without any moral qualm; Burton's description of ageing Eastern women illustrates such an attitude:

> The author [of the *Arabian Nights*] neglects to mention the ugliest part of old-womanhood in the East, long empty breasts like tobacco pouches. In youth, the bosom is beautifully high, arched and rounded, firm as stone to the touch, with the nipples erect and pointing outwards. But after the girl-mother's first child . . . all changes.[79]

Burton's tone here, pretending to aesthetic preoccupation, becomes disturbingly pornographic in its recounting of the visual details of the woman's body: erect nipples firm as stone, resistant in their physical hardness, but unresisting in their nakedness to the trained eye evaluating them.

And this was, after all, the Victorian age's official method of viewing women, reducing them to body, to possession, to physical object. The *Arabian Nights* became a timely collection since it upheld an established idea of womanhood, with the foreignness of the tales excusing their unseemliness, and providing exotic stimulus that was as episodic and as prolific as the Victorian male readership could desire.

When translating from Eastern languages, Burton concentrated on such texts as would have erotic appeal, since eroticism seemed the only interesting thing the East had to offer the West. In the *Kama Sutra* and in *The Perfumed Garden*, Burton went far in confirming the idea that Easterners were highly skilled in sexual matters – the only real skill they seemed to possess. But although Burton liked to suggest that the East could tutor the West in erotic techniques, he could not help feeling disappointment in its sexual manuals; they were not as explicit as he would have desired. In the Introduction to his translation of *The Perfumed Garden*, he complained that the author Shaykh Nefzawi had left out the mention of sodomy and of homosexuality, among other things:

> There might have been given on this subject sound advice, as well with regard to the pleasures mutually enjoyed by women called Tribades. The same silence has been preserved by the author respecting bestiality. Lastly, the sheikh does not mention the pleasures which the mouth or the hand of a pretty woman can give, nor the cunnilingus.[80]

The edition of his translation of *The Perfumed Garden* which he issued in 1886 left Burton dissatisfied. He decided to re-issue the book, adding extensive notes in the process. He referred to this intention in a letter, claiming that a new edition 'will be a marvelous repertory of Eastern wisdom, how Eunuchs are made, and are married, what they do in marriage; female circumcision, the Fellah (Egyptian peasant) copulating with crocodiles, etc.'[81] Already, in his first translation (the second amended one was never published; it was destroyed by Lady Isabel at her husband's death), Burton had included twenty-five extra sexual positions to the ones mentioned by the Arab author. He also added eighteen additional names for the male member, augmenting the list that Nefzawi had supplied. And to the erotic stories recounted in the Arabic text, Burton added four new ones.[82] He was out to out-Nefzawi Nefzawi.

'Eastern wisdom', then, consisted for Burton of sexual wisdom. Although he was well-versed in Arab and Indian cultures, although he had culled a vast store of knowledge from his Eastern travels, Burton chose to present the sum of his experience in one specific mode. His East was the conventional sexual realm of the Western imagination, a realm that could only be depicted, in his age, by an unconventional man. It is therefore not a little ironic to find that someone with the linguistic and intellectual capacities of Burton should, in the end, have helped only to further confirm the myth of the erotic East. The great Seraglio, so deeply entrenched in the European imagination, arrested the perception of even the most gifted of scholars. Its shadow fell heavily on the landscape they travelled through, so that they hardly saw anything at all of the details before them.

3 The Salon's Seraglio

In 1829, in the preface to his poem 'Les Orientales', Victor Hugo mentioned the East's modish attractiveness, saying:

> On s'occupe aujourd'hui beaucoup plus de l'Orient qu'on ne l'a jamais fait. Les études orientales n'ont jamais été poussées si avant. Au siècle de Louis XIV on était Helleniste, maintenant on est Orientaliste.[1]

Europe was charmed by an Orient that shimmered with possibilities, that promised a sexual space, a voyage away from the self, an escape from the dictates of the bourgeois morality of the metropolis. The European reacted to the encounter as a man might react to a woman, by manifesting strong attraction or strong repulsion. E. W. Lane described his first sight of Egypt, the Egypt he had dreamed of since boyhood, thus:

> As I approached the shore, I felt like an Eastern bridegroom, about to lift the veil of his bride, and to see, for the first time, the features that were to charm, or disappoint, or disgust him.[2]

The European was led into the East by sexuality, by the embodiment of it in a woman or a young boy. He entered an imaginary harem when entering the metaphor of the Orient, weighed down by inexpressible longings. His century had pushed women into rigid roles: the leisured middle-class wife who was supposedly dormant sexually, the domestic servant whom labour unsexed, and the prostitute who was burdened with all that the wife was protected from.

The Victorian woman's fate, then, was three-sided, a triple manifestation of the same servitude. The real economic forces that worked to produce such female stereotypes worked also to produce a desire for a different image of women – unburdened by the associations of guilt affixed to wife, servant and prostitute. This new image of women would have to satisfy all the male's contradictory needs; she would have to be angel, whore and confidante at once. She would have to have desires, and indulge in sexual excesses while remaining ethereal.

The Pre-Raphaelite search for such a fantasy of womanhood culminated in Jane Burden. She was made to embody an alternative *ethos*, as this description of her suggests: 'When she came into a room, in her strangely beautiful garments, looking at least eight feet high, the effect was as if she had walked out of an Egyptian tomb at Luxor.'[3] Jane Burden's beauty carried in it a dimension of foreignness: she looked as though she had emerged from another world, a different civilisation, 'an Egyptian tomb'. Her dark and profuse hair, her black brows that met, the aura of mystery that hung upon her like the exotic velvets she wore, all joined in forming an allure that was unfamiliar. Uncorseted, uncommunicative, she exuded an eroticism that was decadent, and 'other'.

The eroticism that the East promised was mysterious and tinged with hints of violence. The Oriental woman was linked, like a primitive goddess, with cycles of the supernatural. Cleopatra possesses knowledge of magic and poisonous prescriptions long before the need for death arises. Scheherazade lives on the edge of the sword, its blade is what her narrative must defeat, its shadow what makes her tale so captivating. Salome's dance is sexual and macabre at once. Her beauty is linked to the darker elements, complicit with the corruption that John the Baptist's words uncover. Her dance is delirium inspiring, and causes the unleashing of evil. Oscar Wilde's interpretation of Salome's murderous desire for Jokanaan's head as the other side of her sexual passion for him indicates the treacherous nature of Eastern sexuality: Salome dances on blood, and kisses the severed head in a frenzy of brutish arousal:

> Ah! I have kissed thy mouth, Jokanaan, I have kissed thy mouth; There was a bitter taste on thy lips. Was it the taste of blood? . . . Nay; but perchance it was the taste of love . . . They say that love hath a bitter taste . . . But what matter? what matter? I have kissed thy mouth.[4]

The dance itself proved to be the undoing of nature; even the moon turned red as Salome danced.[5] Flaubert also described Salome's demented dance in *Hérodias*:

> . . . sur le haut de l'estrade, elle retira son voile . . . puis elle se mit à danser. Ses pieds passaient l'un devant l'autre au rythme de la flûte et d'une paire de crotales, ses bras arrondis appelaient quelqu'un qui s'enfuyait toujours.[6]

The dance became invested with an exhibitionism that fascinated the onlooker: he saw it as a metaphor for the whole East. In the Orientalist paintings of the nineteenth century, it often became a trope for the Orient's abandon, for it seemed to be a dramatically different mode of dancing from its Western counterpart. It was not a social expression only,[7] since the woman (scantily-clad as she was pictured) was there to please the onlooker, who did not participate but watched. The dance could be used as a medium that illustrated what were perceived to be the Orient's qualities. It could portray female nudity, rich and sequestered interiors, jewels, hints of lesbianism, sexual languour and sexual violence; in brief, it encapsulated the painted East.

Just as Neo-Classical painting had been able to portray nudity by placing it in a removed mythological setting, so the Orientalist painters began depicting an explicit sensuality by placing it in a *lieu* that was removed from their contemporary surroundings. This *lieu*, the painted East, appealed to a bourgeois public keen on exoticism.

Nudity had obviously been often depicted in Western painting, and yet the nudes of the Orientalists were startling. Perhaps the mythological context that previous nudes had been placed in had served to mute their impact – Venus, after all, was recognisably mythical. But if the painted woman was not weighted down by mythology, if the onlooker could imagine her to be in the realm of the touchable and possessable, then the barrier of disbelief lifts and the sensuality becomes more explicit and direct.

In pondering the transformations in Rococo space, Norman Bryson speaks of the emergence of the creatural body through 'the classical opposition' (the *logos* of discursive language, the counter-erotic eloquence) in order to gain recognition as spectacle:

For its erotic content to be fully yielded up, the body must be presented to the viewer as though uniquely made to gratify and be consumed in the moment of the glance. All signs that the body has other purposes, another history, are to be suppressed; it cannot even have a setting of its own.[8]

This could apply as aptly to Orientalist tableaux with a difference allowed. The setting as value changes: in the Rococo scene, it is minimalised to the point of negation – thus the cloud atmosphere of the background, the cushioning vapour providing a bed for nymphs and cupids, are there only to better yield their content of body. In the Orientalist interior (and the erotic scenes in this genre almost always depict an interior), the setting is vital to the body it cushions. It is a catalogue of goods, a showpiece of commodities that the viewer might covet. It is a travesty of the depictions of Victorian interiors with their bric-à-brac of industrial wealth, and their fully-clad and demure heroine. The nude or semi-clothed woman in the Orientalist painting is made more erotic by her surroundings of material objects, by the cushions, hangings, sofas, vessels, fans, bottles, garments and musical instruments which the viewer's eye is made to take in. The glance is therefore prolonged in a Baudelairean appreciation of the Oriental interior:

> Les riches plafonds,
> Les miroirs profonds,
> La splendeur orientale,
> Tout y parlerait,
> A l'âme en secret,
> Sa douce langue natale.

In such an interior, the woman is an isolated object, and as such, displaces the set notions of the bourgeois interior. As an object that is usually hidden, cloaked, clothed, masked, the woman's revealed body becomes startling and arousing in contrast with a well-dressed room.

The nineteenth century, a conspicuously consuming era, thirsted for variety in its sexual depictions as it craved a variety of products in its markets. Jacques Bousquet has suggested that this wish for a multiplicity of representations manifested itself in different forms. One was a preoccupation with ugliness, with vampishness as deviation from the accepted norms of the beautiful. Another was a fascination with little girls as a deviation from the norm of the desirable mature woman.[9] And from this hunger for diversity sprang the attractiveness of the foreign woman, racially deviant, erotic because exotic. Thus the cult of dandyism towards the end of the century – which cultivated differentness in an era of uniformity – cultivated as well susceptibility to the foreign. Baudelaire's first voyage to Mauritius provided him with an experience that would set the stage for his desire for the mulatto Jeanne Duval. He watched a black woman being whipped on shore, and recorded that he became sexually excited.[10] He would from then on distinguish between passion and love; he would feel desire for foreign women (usually dark ones), but platonic love for white women who were his superiors socially (like Madame de Sabatier), and who reminded him of his mother.[11] Duval was recreated in hot images; in her hair lurked 'la langoureuse Asie et la brulante Afrique'. She herself is a voyage East, providing sexual possibilities but precluded from respectability. Her dark body for Baudelaire disturbed as it attracted; it was a flower of evil, to be sampled away from the blooms of the bourgeois conservatory.

In a study of dreams prevalent between 1830 and 1870, Bousquet noticed a frequency in those depicting harems or orgies, where the dreamer could possess a multiplicity of women.[12] This type of dream came to be transferred to the artistic *oeuvre*; the multiple gratification that is promised in the dream is barbaric, Oriental. The Orient promised similar transgressions to the waking mind. Raymond Schwab sees Flaubert's usage of the East as literary metaphor as a flight from the prosaic self, from the boredom of the *quotidien*:

Le barbare de Flaubert, c'est une revanche sur un étouffement de cage intérieure, la sanction d'une incapacité à sortir de soi; significatif est le besoin de lier le barbare à l'oriental, pour que les deux mots profitent d'un même prestige.[13]

The imaginary voyage to the Orient began, for Flaubert, long before he actually embarked on his tour of the East. When he finally arrived in Egypt in 1849, he could write that its atmosphere had the nature of a 'rétrouvaille'. The landscape had already been imprinted in his imagination, culled from the Bible and from

Orientalist accounts and paintings. He saw Egypt as a literary prop for his musings: 'ça avait l'air d'un paysage peint, d'un immense décor de théâtre fait exprés pour nous'.[14]

The real voyage for Flaubert served mainly to authenticate the imaginary one. When he arrived in the Orient, he saw an East he had transported with him; one that he would transport back, in piecemeal, in the form of extravagant objects. The Goncourts described Flaubert's Parisian interior, with its found-objects from the voyage East:

> . . . des amulettes recouvertes de la patine vert-de-grisée de l'Egypte . . . deux pieds de momie arrachés par Flaubert aux grottes de Samoun, étranges presse-papiers, mettant au milieu des brochures, leur bronze fauve et la vie figée des muscles humains . . . C'est l'intérieur tout plein d'un gros Orient, et où perce un fonds de barbare dans une nature d'artiste.[15]

The imaginary and extravagant Orient that he coveted yielded Flaubert a wealth of imagery and a host of characters as well. The Queen of Sheba in *La Tentation de Saint Antoine* became invested with the sexuality that Flaubert associated with the East. It is interesting to note that in a book that he rewrote a great many times, the 'Reine de Saba' episode was the one he hardly altered from one version to another. It had pleased him from its first conception.[16] The Queen of Sheba attempts to seduce the hermit with her Oriental guiles, promising endless erotic gratification and as yet unsampled pleasures:

> Je ne suis pas une femme, je suis un monde. Mes vêtements n'ont qu'à tomber, et tu decouvriras sur ma personne une succession de mystères! Si tu posais ton doigt sur mon épaule, ce serait comme une trainée de feu dans tes veines. La possession de la moindre place de mon corps t'emplira d'une joie plus véhémente que la conquête d'un empire. Avance tes lèvres! Mes baisers ont le goût d'un fruit qui se fondrait dans ton coeur.[17]

She is a pastiche of Oriental female prototypes; she dances like Salome, tells stories like Scheherazade, is regal and ridiculous at once like traditional portrayals of Cleopatra:

> Ris donc, bel ermite! ris donc! Je suis très gaie, tu verras! Je

pince de la lyre, je danse comme une abeille, et je sais une foule
d'histoires à raconter, toutes plus divertissantes les unes que les
autres.[18]

Flaubert's description of his encounter with an Arab *courtisane*
sheds light on the way he perceived his encounter with the Orient
more generally:

> Sur l'escalier, en face de nous, la lumière l'entourant et se
> détachant sur le fond bleu, une femme debout, en pantalon
> rose, n'ayant autour du torse qu'une gaze d'un violet foncé. Elle
> venait de sortir du bain, sa gorge dure sentait frais, quelque
> chose comme une odeur de térébenthine sucrée . . .[19]

The onlooker is admitted into the Orient by visual seduction; he
encounters the woman in a state of undress, emerging from the
intimacy of the bath – in a state of pleasing vulnerability. *He* is not
vulnerable: he is male, presumably in full dress, European,
rational (since even when faced with such erotic liability he can
still recount the precise details of the apparition quite coolly), and
armed with language – *he* narrates the encounter in a reflective,
post-facto narrative; *he* creates the Orient.

The Orient, then, is caught in a state of timelessness, crammed
full of incidents remarkable for their curiosity or eroticism, hushed
into silence by its own mysteries, incapable of self-expression,
mute until the Western observer lends it his voice. It is the seraglio
of the imagination disclosing itself, with its veiled women, its blind
musicians, its black eunuchs and jealous princes; it is the
impossible other, the bourgeois drawing-room's secret foil.

When the Goncourt brothers first visited Théophile Gautier in
1863 and made the acquaintance of his two daughters, they
thought them possessed of an 'Oriental' charm well-suited to their
father's Orientalist inclinations.[20] Gautier's flamboyant tastes
and romantic sensibilities had merged to accentuate his attraction
to Eastern things, enveloping him in what V. G. Kiernan called
'Europe's collective day-dream of the Orient'.[21] Gautier had
written to Maxime du Camp of this attraction, confiding: 'Je me
sens mourir d'une nostalgie d'Asie Mineure.'[22] This manifested
itself in a fascination with Oriental objects and Oriental dress.
When he visited Constantinople, Gautier described his Turkish

hostess's garb with a true dandy's eye for the niceties of ornamentation:

> Cette charmante femme dans son costume de fête: dalmatique mi-partie de damas vert et de damas rouge, grandes manches de gaze fendues et laissant voir un bras d'une correction parfaite; large ceinture de velours ornée de plaques de métal et de boules filigranes glissant sur la taille et retenue par la rondeur des hanches comme un ceste antique.[23]

Gautier was a great lover of Orientalist painting,[24] and an enthusiastic critic of it as well. He found this genre's attention to the details of a rapidly-vanishing scene highly laudable:

> Les artistes, pressentant que cette pittoresque barbarie va bientôt disparaître devant notre plate et laide civilisation, s'empressent à l'envie d'en multiplier les portraits. Dans vingt ans d'ici, les Turcs qui voudront savoir quels costumes portaient leurs pères ne les retrouveront que dans les tableaux de Decamps.[25]

Thus these paintings were seen as repositories of the Orient's qualities, of its 'pittoresque barbarie'. The gorgeousness of the images became official documents of the age's fantasies; the real East was petrified in their details. When Gautier saw Prosper Marilhat's 'La Place de l'Esbekieh au Caire' exhibited in 1834, its effect on him was decisive – he had found his Orient:

> Aucun tableau ne fit sur moi une impression plus profonde et plus longtemps vibrante. J'aurais peur d'être taxé d'exagération en disant que la vue de cette peinture me rendit malade et m'inspira la nostalgie de l'Orient où je n'avais jamais mis les pieds. Je crus que je venais de connaître ma véritable patrie et, lorsque je détournais les yeux de l'ardente peinture, je me sentais exilé.[26]

The Orientalist painters depicted an opulent East from imported trinkets which served as props in the *atelier*. They recreated in their studios the cave of Ali Baba they had read about as children. They also added the necessary objects of violence to depict what they imagined to be a particularly violent East. Gautier's description of Chasseriau's *atelier* illustrates this vogue:

> Les yatagans, les kanjars, les poignards, les pistolets circassiens, les fusils arabes, les vieilles lames de Damas nicklées de verset du Coran, les armes à feu enjolivées d'argent et de corail, tout ce charmant luxe barbare se groupait en trophées le long des murs.[27]

Daggers, swords, knives, pistols; fire arms that represented an explosive and dangerous place where murder was a simple occurrence, where barbaric cruelty and opulence displayed themselves openly. Visiting another Orientalist painter's studio, Gautier's literary imagination provided him with the ready scenes of Eastern criminality to animate the space created by the presence of so many exotic objects: 'Cette chambre pourrait servir de fond à quelque scène de jalousie et de meurtre; le sang ne ferait tâche sur ces tapis d'une pourpre sombre.'[28] And Gautier's perception of an Orient where gore and gems went hand in hand, where blood did not show a stain on the deep purple of Persian rugs, recurred like an insistent theme through the most popular of Orientalist *tableaux*.

Eugène Delacroix's 'La Mort de Sardanapale' (Plate 1) was painted in 1827 before he actually made the journey East. It contains the stock images of Europe's Orient, culled from Byron's popular poem of that name. An Oriental despot sits enthroned on his luxurious bed (with its fantastic heads of elephants and its crimson drapery) detachedly watching all his earthly possessions being destroyed. His naked concubines are being stabbed to death by three dark villains, and his horse is being dragged away. All is chaotic, the brushstroke depicting the scene is an aptly 'romantic' and agitated one, while the canvas is crammed full of dramatic detail and incident, leaving no restful vacuum for the gaze. The violence of the narrative is linked with its eroticism; indeed, the female bodies in the throes of death are made to take on positions of languor, of sexual abandon. Their dying becomes exotic spectacle, voyeuristically observed by both Sardanapalus and the onlooker. The scene yields an opulence of gems (the women are all heavily bejewelled: they wear bracelets, ankle bracelets, necklaces, tiaras, rings, earrings) and of bodies. The opulence of

the East is manifest in these painted gems. Gustave Moreau
covered his many depictions of Salome with jewels (and he
painted her with a frequency that was obssessive). She was the
decadent foil to the hair shirt of John the Baptist, the evilness of
material wealth and its attractiveness too. Wilde's description of
Herod's gems mirrors this ancient association of East with
treasure:

> In a coffer of nacre I have three wondrous turquoises. He who
> wears them on his forehead can imagine things which are not,
> and he who carries them in his hand can turn the fruitful
> woman into a woman who is barren . . . I have mantles that
> have been brought from the land of Seres, and bracelets decked
> about with carbuncles and with jade that come from the city of
> Euphrates.[29]

In 1832, Delacroix visited Morocco, which inspired a series of
paintings, among them the 'Femmes d'Alger'. But the literary
Orient continued to provide Delacroix with his subject-matter,
even after he had come into actual contact with the East. Three
years before he died, he was obviously still preoccupied with
themes from the *Arabian Nights* as the entry in his *Journal* for 23
December 1860 makes clear:

> Sujet des *Mille et Une Nuits*: le sultan Shariar, revenant pour dire
> adieu à sa femme, la trouve dans les bras d'un de ses officiers. Il
> tire son sabre, etc. . . . Le roi des îles Noires (dans l'histoire du
> pêcheur) furieux de la tendresse de sa femme pour le noir, son
> amant, qu'il avait lui-même blessé et qui est là couché, tire son
> sabre pour la tuer: elle l'arrête par son geste et le rend moitié
> homme, moitié marbre.[30]

This vision of the East had not evolved from the one already
portrayed in 'La Mort de Sardanapale'; it was still the baroque
instance of sexual violence that fascinated Delacroix – the sword
drawn in jealousy, the passionate crime.

The despotic Orient of the Western imagination guarded its
secrets closely. An image that recurs again and again in
Orientalist painting is the figure of the guard, most often a black
man, blocking the entrance into the harem, the palace, the
mosque, or, more completely, the East itself. Gérôme's 'Le Garde

du Sérail' (Plate 2) painted in 1859 is a dramatic example of this sort of depiction. The man's expression is both unsympathetic and brutal, and his dagger, axe and pistol are daunting. Even the colour of his robe is fiery, as if to give warning of coming too near. He is the dramatic fixture that completes the door of the seraglio – without him, it would have been a mere thoroughfare, but with him, it becomes the most impenetrable passageway. The women who wait behind it can never be seen, let alone touched. This is Europe's seraglio: the dead hand of jealousy without, and the potential for endless pleasure within.

Ludwig Deutsch's 'Le Garde Nubien' (Plate 3) of 1895 is a more subtle construction than Gérôme's. Here is the same despotic Orient beautified rather than villainised. The black man here is statuesque; his features are finer, his expression more passive, his body in a posture of formal ease. Even his arms are aesthetically pleasing, their ornate gold in sharp contrast with the previous painting's dull brown. But nevertheless the guard remains a barrier to movement: the eye travels to the stylised door behind him, left temptingly ajar. No further entrance is allowed, for this is an illustration of the closedness of the East. It offers great wealth of surface detail but no real depth. There is only the gorgeous triangle of column, guard and door to curtail the wandering gaze. The photorealism of many Orientalist paintings is remarkable here as well; this seems to be a frozen instance of reality presented to the viewer. (Indeed, it is interesting to note that photography at this time was recreating the same tropes of Orientalist painting: the early photographers of the Near East, Bonfils in particular, presented the audience with the *poses plastiques* of odalisques – in this case, Bedouin or Jewish beauties – or European models in Oriental dress, in order to link their new techniques harmoniously with those of genre painting. Bonfils's photographs of ruins had, for a model, the stylised lithographs of David Roberts.)

Henri Regnault's 'Exécution sans jugement sous les rois maures' (Plate 4) of 1870 depicts a killing, the title giving it 'historical' validity: a guard has just executed a man who resembles him in colour, stature and facial features. He looks down unmoved at the severed head as he wipes the blood from the body on his sleeve. The dripping blood forms shapes that parody the muted arabesque design of the background. The guard's powerful muscles bulge, his massive figure in sharp contrast to the soft lines of his tunic. The red of the blood is transfused into diffuse shades: the orange that bathes the whole scene; the pink robe that the guard wears which deepens into blood colour again between his feet, so that he seems to be wading in blood; and the red belt that is wrapped around the dead man's waist. The guard is made more imposing since he is seen by the viewer from below: he looms at the top of the stairs, his sword at neck-level. No other figure in the painting is there to witness the scene; it has been committed in secret, with little emotion, a killing without judgement as befits a capriciously cruel Orient.

The villain in Orientalist painting is almost always depicted as very dark or as black. In a painting entitled 'The Prisoner' (Plate 5) painted by Filippo Baratti in 1883, two dark men appear to be relishing the humiliation of a frail old white man, who is bound and at their mercy. The roles are polarised here, for the painters of this genre could not conceive of white and black as equals – one had always to be at the other's mercy, even when they both fell into the category of 'Orientals'. This follows into depictions of men and women, as we shall soon see.

The villainy of Oriental men is aggravated by the fact that they are portrayed as traders in female bodies. They are the cruel captors who hold women in their avaricious grasp, who use them as chattels, as trading-goods, with little reverence for them as human beings. This idea was highly important in distinguishing between the barbarity of the Eastern male and the civilised behaviour of the Western male. One tied women up and sold them at slave auctions; the other revered them and placed them on pedestals. The European (and the Englishman in particular) cherished the notion of his gentlemanliness among savages. It was one added way of convincing himself that he was born to rule over them. As Mark Girouard has suggested, the sources of imperialism and the sources of the Victorian code of the gentleman were so intertwined that they were often indistinguishable from each other, and affected the way the Empire was run.[31]

Slave-market scenes of varying kinds were one of the main narrative stays of Orientalist painting. Edwin Long's highly popular 'The Babylonian Slave Market' fetched a record price when it was exhibited for sale in London in 1875. John Faed's 'Bedouin exchanging a slave for armour' (Plate 6) of 1857 illustrates a particular kind of exchange: a bedouin brings an almost entirely naked slave-girl into the stall of a seller of swords.

The bedouin's dramatic draperies form a strong contrast with the girl's exposed breasts. The details of her body are there to be inspected by both the merchant and the painting's viewer. They yield up her worth, her equivalent in armour. Her expression is a piteous one, as she watches the merchant's face to remark the decision that will seal her fate. She herself is completely helpless; naked, bound, female, and a slave.

One of the most famous slave-market scenes is Gérôme's 'Le Marché d'Esclaves' (Plate 7) (no date) which is mainly an excuse for portraying female nudity in a more startling setting than the archetypal harem scene. The spectator is drawn into the midst of the mechanics of slave-purchasing. He faces a group of men (on the right hand side) who are the would-be-purchasers. The man in green, whose overwhelming garb sets off the slave's humiliating nakedness, tests the girl's teeth to check her health, prodding his fingers into her mouth with a hand almost as large as her whole head. The girl has been undressed for inspection by the ghoulish-looking man on the left still holding her head veil, who is presumably her owner. She is a carcass, almost, her skin's colour and her facial expression give the impression that she is dead. Like the dead dog in the background on the left, she is an insignificant victim of this East where lives come cheap. Four other victims await their turns for inspection, still huddled in their veils. The purchasers provide the only colour plane in the painting; the background is otherwise drab, dark: the windows that give on to the courtyard are gaping eyes that see nothing, openings into a further darkness, symbols of a complete hopelessness.

Although Westerners claimed to be horrified by the slave-trade, depictions of it were coveted by a genteel bourgeois public. The image of the captive beauty appealed to patriarchal urges of domination, and to imperialistic urges more generally. Both Lane and Baker kept slaves whom they transformed in true Pygmalion style and later married. Gerard de Nerval recounts that he purchased a Javanese woman to keep house for him in Cairo, describing with pleasure her accommodating nature and her docility. He claims to have been scandalised, however, when offering to set her free on the eve of his departure, she begged him to sell her again in the hope that her chances might improve.[32]

Oriental males, as we have seen, are almost always portrayed as predatory figures in Orientalist painting. They are mostly shown as ugly or loathsome, in contrast to the women who are beautiful

and voluptuous. This leaves the woman free for the abduction of
the viewer's gaze since she is not attached within the painting,
being mismatched with a male who is her obvious inferior. Thus,
she must desire to be saved from her fate in some way. By such
projection, the European fantasised about the Eastern woman's
emotional dependency on him. This appealed to his sense of
himself as romantic hero. Victor Hugo had an Arab woman voice
exactly such sentiments to the departing European:

> Si tu ne reviens pas, songe un peu
>   quelquefois
> Aux filles du désert, soeur à la douce
>   voix,
> Qui dansent pieds nus sur la dune;
> Ô beau jeune homme blanc, bel oiseau
>   passager,
> Souviens-toi, car peut-être,
>   ô rapide étranger,
> Ton souvenir reste à plus d'une![33]

Pierre Loti's *Aziyadé* describes the native woman's surrender to a
white man – not because he is powerful and she is forced to serve
him – but because he has seduced her with his personal charm and
holds her in willing captivity. When the story's hero, an English
officer (also) named Loti, is about to depart with his regiment,
Aziyadé loses all force, falls ill, suffers inconsolable anguish, and
after his departure, dies. Loti the officer (like his namesake the
author) had come East and had been entranced by the love of a
passionate Oriental, by the gratification of his senses in all
possible ways (perfumes, foods, narcotics, music): 'Le bruit
déchirant de cette musique, la fumée aromatisée du narguilé
amenaient doucement l'ivresse, cette ivresse orientale qui est
l'anéantissement du passé et l'oubli des heures sombres de
la vie.'[34]

This romantic dependency that the European liked to cherish
was only a sublimated form of Eastern womens' real dependency
on Western men. All Easterners were ultimately dependent in the
colonial power balance, but women and young boys especially so.
Thus they served as the colonial world's sex symbols, its
accommodating objects. Since the Victorian imagination could
not conceive of female eroticism divorced from female servitude;

since in the core of nineteenth-century sexuality there lurked all the conflicts of power and powerlessness, wealth ·and poverty, mastery and slavehood, the spectacle of subject women (and boys) could not but be exciting. The Western male could possess the native woman by force of his dominion over her native land; she was subjugated by his wealth, his military might, and his access to machinery. She was his colonial acquisition, but one that he pretended enjoyed his domination and would mourn his departure. (In the same manner, the eminent Victorian Arthur J. Munby urged a poor worker named Hannah Culwick to keep a diary in which she was to note graphic details of her life of degradation – details which he found exciting. He made her wear a leather strap on her wrist as a sign of her bondage to him. In the same vein, the upper classes often found their domestics erotic; in some brothels, clients would ask prostitutes to dress as servants. The more dependent economically the woman was, the more erotic she appeared.)

The desirable woman in Orientalist painting was hardly ever 'foreign' looking. She conformed closely with conventional standards of European beauty. The more desirable prototypes were Circassian (the fair-skinned descendants of the Circassian subjects of the Ottoman Empire) since they were exotic without being unappetisingly dark. The light-haired Circassians were made (as the European liked to imagine) precisely for sensual gratification. Gerard de Nerval describes his encounter with one of these beauties in the following manner:

> La Circassienne, qui paraissait jouer le rôle de khanoum ou maitresse, s'avance vers nous, prit une cuiller de vermeil qu'elle trempa dans des confitures de roses, et me presenta la cuiller devant la bouche avec une sourire des plus gracieux.[35]

The nuance of sexual gratification is linked with the offer of a delicacy; the Circassian extends a spoon filled with rose marmalade to Nerval, passing herself into the offering as she smiles graciously. She is both offerer and offering, herself the delicacy to be sampled.

Lecomte de Nouy's 'L'Esclave Blanche' (Plate 8) of 1888 idealises the Circassian beauty in the manner that was fashionable in *salons* exhibitions. The woman is unaware of being watched, and thus the voyeuristic atmosphere of most of the paintings of this genre is made even more apparent here. The woman is enjoying a delicate meal served on ornate china. In order for the fantasy to be complete, she appears naked, disclosed from her garments like the segments of orange that await her consumption. She is all soft curves: her feet, her fingers, shoulders, belly, chin, mouth and nose all drawn in the same curvaceous manner. This is in strong contrast to the angularity of the black servants in the background; they are made for work, while she can only labour in love.

Lecomte de Nouy had gained attention as a painter of Classical ruins. He was a painstaking and sober craftsman whose depictions of Greek temples and amphitheatres were a scholar's dream. Later on in his career, however, he turned Orientalist; with this shift in subject matter, there was a distinct shift in style and technique. His paintings became less precise and more emotional – his *néo-grec* works had almost been archaeological documents, whereas his Eastern *tableaux* were fantastic collages of opulence, languor and eroticism, in which he used light to achieve melodrama and often oppressive sadness. Lecomte de Nouy's Orient was a purely literary one; he culled his inspiration from the popular *oeuvres* of the day: for example, his famous 'Ramses dans son harem' of 1885 was an illustration of Théophile Gautier's *Le Roman de la Momie*. In the same manner, Ingres (who had never set foot in the Orient, but whose Odalisques became the archetypes of Eastern eroticism) depended on the letters of Lady Montagu and the writings of Montesquieu for his inspiration.

In the real East, for those painters who did make the journey, there was inspiration enough. William Makepeace Thackeray realised this quickly as he ambled about Cairo on his extended Grand Tour: 'There is a fortune to be made for painters in Cairo ... I never saw such a variety of architecture, of life, of picturesqueness, of brilliant colour, of light and shade. There is a picture in every street, and at every bazaar stall.'[36] But despite such wealth of images, there was something that overpowered the European artists and induced them to offer a variation on a theme. Very few of the Orientalist painters were able to offer a narrative-free depiction of the scenes they were witness to. They narrated the East while painting it, they transformed it into metaphor and myth. They offered Europe what Europe wished to see. In fact, the ambitious and serious landscape painters never gained the popularity instantly accorded the more fantastic

Orientalists. Edward Lear, for instance, that inexhaustible and witty traveller, was out of tune with the 'Orient' in demand. His careful watercolours created little enthusiasm, having nothing of the sensationalistic about them. He died an unhappy and unrewarded artist, writing to Lady Waldegrave in 1868 that he had only managed to 'topographize [his] life'.[37]

J. F. Lewis followed a different path from Lear's, choosing to depict from the very start an Orientalist's Orient. He had fallen under the spell of a literary Orient, and had published a collection of engravings entitled *Illustrations of Constantinople* (1837) three years before he actually visited that city. Lewis, in the manner of Lane, decided to take up temporary residence in Cairo, and rented a house there away from the local Franks. Thackeray, who visited him during this period, found him attired in 'a pair of trousers which would make a set of dresses for an English family'. Thackeray mused over the transformation of one who had once been renowned in Regent Street for 'the faultlessness of his boots and cravats, and the brilliancy of his waistcoats and kid gloves'. No doubt, back in London, the painter's 'neglected sisters tremble to think their Frederick is going about with a great beard and a crooked sword, dressed up like an odious Turk'.[38] Thackeray eyed his surroundings for other incriminating signs of Lewis's having 'turned Turk'; peering into the courtyard, his detective sense was soon rewarded:

> There were wooden lattices to those arched windows, through the diamonds of one of which I saw two of the most beautiful, enormous, ogling, black eyes in the world, looking down upon the interesting stranger.[39]

On pressing his host for an explanation, Thackeray is informed that the apparition he had glimpsed was Lewis's very plain cook.

Lewis was not, however, insensitive to the Oriental beauty. He painted idealised Circassians within the confines of the 'harem-scene' genre popular during the period. He produced a great many variations on this particular theme, fascinated by the idea of disclosing to the viewer what lay behind the seraglio's closed doors. His interiors pay a minute attention to detail. He obviously revelled in reproducing the intricacies of arabesque designs as they appeared on woodwork, fabric and tile. His paintings show a considerable skill in the handling of light patterns, in the treatment of different textures, and in the observation of objects unique to Eastern interiors. Yet despite having given care to such recreation of an observed reality, Lewis could not resist peopling the painted space with a multiplicity of sensual women, as if to cater to a prefabricated trope. In 'The Harem' (Plate 9), for example, painted in 1850, he presents within a typical Cairene interior of the nineteenth century a stereotypical depiction of an Arab male surrounded by his wives. The same interior is again recreated in 'Harem Life in Constantinople' (1857) and in the famous 'Siesta' (1876). In these paintings, the male is absent, and the women are whiling the time away in chatting, dressing, sleeping, as they await his return. The women in Orientalist paintings never work as they do in mainstream depictions of them in Western art. They do not embroider, or cook, or sew, or pray – they hardly perform any duty at all. They simply prepare and adorn themselves for the absent male, and they wait.

In 1862, in his Paris *atelier*, the ageing Jean Auguste Dominique Ingres finished painting a round oil which he entitled 'Le Bain Turc' (Plate 10). The painting consists of twenty-six nude women, sampling the varied pleasures of a fantastic Turkish bath. A musician with her back turned to the viewer leads the eye into the scene. The back is turned thus not as a social affront, but as indication that the woman is oblivious to any audience excepting the one before her, within the painting. That inner audience is also unaware of being watched; none of the women look out towards the viewer. They are enclosed within a private space, one which they think impervious to any outsider's gaze.

The round shape of the painting continues the theme of femaleness, by picking up the roundness of breasts, bellies, thighs depicted within. It also evokes the roundness of a scene as perceived through the round aperture of a keyhole. This voyeurism is an intrinsic part of the painting, for the onlooker has been presented with a means of gazing into a forbidden East. He enters a world of sexual abandon; he sees without being seen.

The women in the painting all appear to be cloned from one model, as if depictions of one woman in an endless variety of poses. They are intertwined in love-postures, hinting at lesbian relationships. No bathing activity is actually visible: the bath here seems to be an occasion for undressing and dallying. The painting is an obvious collage of the hackneyed themes of Eastern sensuality; the women fondling each other, the perfumes, the incense, the music – all convey the endless potential for erotic gratification of such a *lieu*. The eroticism becomes, unintentionally, no doubt, a parody of itself. For the compilation of bodies in such numerous mass disturbs without arousing. It is a surplus which satiates.

Such portraits, in wishing to convey the East, described more accurately, Europe. They portrayed the repressiveness of its social codes, and the heavy hand of its bourgeois morality. The gaze into the Orient had turned, as in a convex mirror, to reflect the Occident that had produced it.

4 Doughty Travellers

In his biography of Richard Burton, Byron Farwell begins by stating that 'the explorer is always a civilized man; exploration is an advanced intellectual concept'.[1] Therefore, he argues, it is a concept unknown to primitive peoples, and one that remains incomprehensible to women. This observation points to qualities that are intrinsic to exploration – especially the kind of exploration that concerns us here, that which produces travel narrative; first, that it is linked to politics, a more accurate term than Farwell's 'civilisation', and second, that it is patriarchal, even when undertaken by women such as Hester Stanhope or Gertrude Bell who were capable enough of grasping 'an advanced intellectual concept'.

The explorer is preoccupied with what he sees, with arranging the elements of the information he has gleaned till they are contained within a comprehensible pattern. An Adam-like figure, he names all that he encounters in the hitherto uncharted (uncharted by him or his countrymen) chaos of the remote. From the moment of this naming ritual, the observed elements acquire significance and begin to be.

The counterpart to the real explorer, the heroic traveller in mythological fiction, often commences his journey from a point that is not merely a geographical location, but a stronghold of culture and tradition. The journey embarked on is a movement away from this starting point towards experiences in situations deeply alien to the traveller's original environment. In order for the journey to be heroic, the traveller must return home having seen and overcome the alien world he has passed through, with the precepts of his culture intact, his moral vision unaltered, and his personality strengthened and confirmed by its trials. Thus *Gulliver's Travels* ironically transforms the archetypal heroic voyage by making the hero return deeply altered in vision. *He* has become the alien, shunning his former companions, no longer able

1. Eugène Delacroix:
   La Mort de Sardanapale, 1827–8
   (Musée de Louvre, Paris)

2. Jean-Léon Gérôme:

3. Ludwig Deutsch:

4. Henri Regnault:
    Exécution sans Jugement, 1870
    (Musée de Louvre, Paris)

5. Filippo Baratti:
The Prisoner, 1883
(Fine Art Society Ltd, London)

6. John Faed:
   Bedouin Exchanging a Slave for Armour, c. 1857
   (Fine Art Society Ltd, London)

7. Jean-Léon Gérôme:
    Le Marché d'Esclaves, no date
    (Sterling and Francine Clark Institute, Williamstown, Mass.,
    USA)

8. Jean-Jules-Antoine, Lecomte de Nouy:
L'Esclave Blanche, 1888
(Musée des Beaux-Arts, Nantes)

9. John Frederick Lewis:
The Hhareem, c. 1850
(The Victoria and Albert Museum, London)

10. Jean Auguste Dominique Ingres:
Le Bain Turc, 1862
(Musée de Louvre, Paris)

to tolerate even the smell of his own family. He has become an aberration; the voyage has overpowered him completely – it has robbed him of his *pays*.

The traveller to the East in the literature of the West has closely followed the pattern of the heroic voyage. Disraeli's Tancred, for example, starts out from his parental estate armed with that location's code of conduct and outlook. He heads for the East in order to become enlightened, but as his journey progresses, he gradually becomes an enlightener instead. He imports to the chaotic and emotive landscape that he travels through the restraint and the authoritative morality of his upbringing. He emerges from the East mellowed, but virtually unchanged. He has endured the alien without suffering any fragmentation of his being.

The nineteenth-century Britain that produced the fictional Tancred also produced real travellers who shared many characteristics with their literary counterparts. They had commenced their voyage long before the actual physical embarkation. They had absorbed from their education, from the readings of their youth, a great many of the qualities with which they were predestined to endow the East. And although the Victorian traveller was keen to explore the world, he most often did not succeed in transcending his cultural preconditioning in the process. William Hazlitt, in 'On Going on a Journey', broods on this very difficulty of evading the familiar:

> There is undoubtedly a sensation in travelling into foreign parts that is to be had nowhere else: but it is more pleasing at the time than lasting. It is too remote from our habitual associations to be a common topic of discourse or reference, and like a dream or another state of existence, does not piece into our daily modes of life.[2]

These 'habitual associations', threatened by the journey to foreign parts, must be safeguarded in some way to ensure the ease of the traveller. Hazlitt suggests the taking of a companion from one's own country with one, since there 'is an involuntary antipathy in the mind of an Englishman to foreign manners and notions that requires the assistance of social sympathy to carry it off'. He elaborates on the sense of alienness that the traveller feels when cut off from his own language and his own kind. The further from England one goes, the more necessary one's Englishness becomes to one:

> A person would almost feel stifled to find himself in the deserts of Arabia without friends or countrymen . . . In such situations, so opposite to all one's ordinary train of ideas, one seems a species by one's self, a limb torn off from society, unless one can meet with instant fellowship and support.[3]

If the English traveller travelled without a companion, he could at least fall back on the testimony of previous travellers in order to avoid a sense of isolation in the countries he passed through. This testimony perpetuated a unified documentation of the East, and was hardly ever reappraised. Since Europe was seen as a foil to the Orient, and endowed with all conceivable positive attributes, the East was judged on its similarity to or difference from the West. To be less like it was to remain in a state of otherness, of inferiority, to become more like Europe was to progress.

Officialdom in general, and in particular institutions such as the Royal Geographical Society, the East India Company, and (as the rage for antiquities evolved from a private passion to a national instinct) the British Museum, encouraged the efforts of travellers to describe the countries that they journeyed in. This fitted in with the general appetite for knowledge, the Victorian age's addiction to enquiry and desire for intellectual control. Thus the East became a place where one could decipher alphabets or discover landmarks, and push back still further the boundaries of Empire in all possible ways, and the individual traveller's vision, by nature of its being subject to his membership of a colonial society – whether he upheld the precepts of colonialism or not – became a medium that ultimately served to forge the myths of imperialism, since it tutored public opinion in the West in a particular manner. The materials of travel perception were wrought into an augmentable tradition, one that could be continually consolidated by individual writers. This tradition became powerfully operative in the forging of cultural definitions.

The idea of penetrating into the East preoccupied the British travellers of the Victorian period. Many thought that living as similar a life as possible to that lived by Easterners was the best way to unravel mysteries. Lane, for example, stressed the fact that he had chosen to live in an Arab section of Cairo, in order to observe Muslim life more closely:

> I have associated, almost exclusively, with Muslims, of various ranks in society: I have lived as they live, conforming with their general habits; and in order to make them familiar and unreserved towards me on every subject, have always avowed my opinion . . . While from the dress which I have found most convenient to wear, I am generally mistaken in public for a Turk.[4]

Lane wished to disguise all aspects of his Englishness in all the ways open to him, by adopting new dress, new opinions, and a new name. Edward William Lane, Esquire, was now Mansoor Effendi. Many of the disguised English travellers would also symbolically change their names: Burton assumed the title of 'Mirza Abdallah of Bushire' (a title that he changed with each change in the nuances of his disguise), Doughty chose the name 'Khalil' since he believed it the closest Arabic equivalent to 'Charles', and Lawrence was content with the mispronunciation of his name by the bedouins – 'Aurens' – which to his ears sounded sufficiently arabicised.

The disguise permitted its wearer to move from one racial category to another as if by magic. This move, with its accompanying implication of moving downward in human worth and in social acceptance, was stimulating as a game; in reality, however, it was reflective of the severe regimentation of Victorian society, where any serious divergence from the consecrated hierarchies would lead to complete ostracism. Moving from one racial category to another, shedding European clothes for Oriental garb became a pleasant pastime for the traveller. However, no European ever wished to actually *become* Oriental in emulating Oriental speech, dress, and habits. Nor would any European prefer the society of Orientals to that of Europeans unless, as in Lane and Burton's case, that society helped in furthering his goal of accumulating facts. West and East, therefore, continued as two distinct and unmeeting entities, between which only the most superficial ties could be had.

The disguise, then, came to serve as leisured play-acting for the wealthy. It appealed to a jaded Victorian imagination by making a journey East more exotic, and it seemed to allow the traveller a deeper access to a cloistered world which he thought guarded its secrets closely. The more difficult the journey could be made to appear, the more exhilarating would become the actual act of embarkation. Burton's journey to Meccah is a particularly good example of such a fascination with danger. One of his self-confessed reasons for embarking on the 'pilgrimage' was the need to put his powers of disguise to the ultimate and most dangerous test: could he pass for a Muslim, risking his life if discovered, and reach that most sequestered of cities, Meccah? This was the real challenge, and in it lay the impetus for the journey. He speaks of the 'gratified pride' that he was filled with when he managed to reach his destination:

> There at last it lay, the bourn of my long and weary Pilgrimage, realising the plans and hopes of many and many a year. The mirage medium of Fancy invested the huge catafalque and its gloomy pall with peculiar charms ... the view was strange, unique – and how few have looked upon the celebrated shrine! I may truly say that, of all the worshippers who clung weeping to the curtain, or pressed their beating hearts to the stone, none felt for the moment a deeper emotion than did the Haji from the far-north ... But, to confess humbling truth, theirs was the high feeling of religious enthusiasm, mine was the ecstasy of gratified pride.[5]

One of the pleasurable aspects of the disguise is that it affords both the wearer and his audience with entertainment. It is a game of skills, a competitive sport; the disguised person is playing at being Arab. If he played artfully enough, he might even beat the native at his own game. Some Westerners were thus able to achieve a curious transformation whereby the romance and admiration so long surrounding the bedouin became transferred to them. They became, as Peter Brent has argued, 'bedouin-extraordinary, super-Arabs'.[6]

The disguised person enjoyed the effect that his going native had on his compatriots. Burton recounts how he was cursed by two colleagues in the Indian Army (who had not recognised him) and called an 'upstart nigger' for venturing too near. Lawrence describes Allenby's bemusement at the sight of a 'little bare-footed silk-skirted man'; highly confused, he glanced sideways at him, unsure 'how much was genuine performer, and how much charlatan'.

The disguise was also used as a political weapon of sorts, a means of infiltrating into a society in order to gain information. James Silk Buckingham, for instance, in his *Travels in Palestine* of 1821 (which he dedicated to the then Governor-General of India), disguised himself as an Egyptian Fellah and attempted to learn Arabic:

> Through the greater part of the country I passed as a native of it, wearing the dress and speaking the language of the Arabs, and by these means commanding a free intercourse with the people in their most unguarded moments, and opening sources of information which would otherwise have been inaccessible.[7]

Burton, as he was travelling to Meccah disguised as a wandering Pashan, was approached by an Indian who, in patriotic complicity, informed him of the riots about to be scheduled against the British in the Indian provinces. Burton wasted no time in telegraphing this choice item back to British Headquarters.

Thus the mode of disguise became the classic method through which the British related to the Arab world. The mode itself, as Leila Ahmed has suggested, 'perpetuates in its very lineaments the condition of enmity, aggression, and rivalry that subsisted between the West and Islam when that mode was first devised: by the West. Consequently, aggression and cultural rivalry are always latent in it.'[8]

The disguised travellers did not merge with the culture they were parodying: the more like that culture's inhabitants they appeared in dress and manner, the more distinct they felt themselves to be, the more convinced they became of their own superiority. This feeling led them to offer prescriptions on the handling of natives. Here is Burton's recipe for dealing with Egyptians: 'They are to be managed as Sir Charles Napier governed Sind – by keeping a watchful eye upon them, a free administration of military law, disarming the population, and forbidding large bodies of men to assemble.'[9] And here Lawrence's prescription for handling Arabs:

> The beginning and ending of the secret of handling Arabs is unremitting study of them. Keep always on your guard: never

say any unconsidered thing. Watch yourself and your
companions all the time: hear all that passes, search out what is
going on beneath the surface, read their characters, discover
their tastes and their weaknesses, and keep everything you find
out to yourself.[10]

This passage reflects the strong sense of separateness that the
English felt in relation to the peoples they travelled amongst.
Lawrence's case was a particularly extreme one, and the more
closely he came to be identified with the Arabs, the more alien he
felt himself to be: 'I was sent to the Arabs as a stranger, unable to
think their thoughts or subscribe to their beliefs . . . If I could not
assume their character, I could at least conceal my own.'[11]

The deception practised by the English traveller – of seeming
Oriental but being Occidental – sometimes produced an
emotional fragmentation that disturbed and frightened.
Lawrence describes this phenomenon:

In my case, the efforts for these years to live in the dress of
Arabs, and imitate their mental foundation, quitted me of my
English self . . . At the same time I could not sincerely take on
the Arab skin: it was an affectation only . . . Sometimes these
selves would converse in the void; and then madness was very
near, as I believe it would be near the man who could see things
through the veils at once of two customs, two educations, two
environments.[12]

Out of context, the passage's melancholy and doubt are
poignantly impressive. But such feelings hardly pursued
Lawrence to the degree such expression would have one believe.
Indeed, he *knew* that he was utterly distinct from the darker
humans whose lot he shared for a brief moment. Describing his
repulsion at the blacks among the tribes, he wrote: 'Their faces,
being clearly different from our own, were tolerable; but it hurt
that they should possess exact counterparts of all our bodies.'[13]
Lawrence's distress, as these lines suggest, was at the degree of
sameness that he inevitably shared with the natives in possessing
a human body, a feeling almost identical to Gulliver's resentment
at the Yahoos for having bodies that resemble his own.

The Englishman felt himself to be mentally as well as physically
superior to those he travelled amongst. This imposed upon him an

acute white man's burden that bid him try and enlighten them. It was in such a spirit that Lawrence took it upon himself to 'lead' the Arabs, incapable as he thought them to take their destiny into their own hands:

> I meant to make a new nation, to restore a lost influence, to give twenty million Semites the foundations on which to build an inspired dream-palace of their national thought.[14]

Lawrence might have felt, at times, the absurdity of such claims. He felt the grotesqueness of his situation, how the playing of the master, by force of irony, often enslaves its player.

> A man who gives himself to be a possession of aliens leads a Yahoo life, having bartered his soul to a brute-master. He is not of them. He may stand against them, persuade himself of a mission, batter and twist them into something which they, of their own accord, would not have been. Then he is exploiting his own environment to press them out of theirs.[15]

Lawrence's Arabs, then, are aliens, and commerce with them is perilous since one must either force them into submission or become enslaved to their perversity. The outsider must 'batter and twist' them into something 'which they, of their own accord, would not have been'. Such drastic measures, however, may sometimes backfire, leaving him in a frightening void where his identity is obscured; he has not mastered them, nor have they converted him. He remains thus, condemned to a Yahoo life of degradation.

The journey Eastward (and the desert journey in particular) provided an alternative self for the English traveller to inhabit, one that he could put aside once it had provided him with the necessary distraction. A haven from the bourgeois parlour, it was a place where inhibitions and social obligations could be shed. E. W. Lane went East to escape such confines, and he was soon 'warped to Orientalism' in Doughty's phrase. He took back with him his Nafeesah and his *nargilah*, and sat cross-legged on chairs at dinner parties, to the consternation of his hosts. The East had been his career in Disraeli's sense, and he was unable to retire from it. Burton, stifled by the sedentary existence of European life, wrote from the dull diplomatic circle in Trieste of the desert's charms, falling into sentimental effusion:

> From my dull and commonplace and 'respectable' surroundings, the Jinn bore me at once to the land of my predilection, Arabia. Again I stood under the diaphanous skies, in air as glorious as aether, whose every breath raises men's spirits like sparkling wine. Once more I saw . . . the homely and rugged features of the scene into a fairy-land lit with a light which never shines on other soils or seas. Then would appear the woolen tents, low and black, of the true Badawin, mere dots in the boundless waste . . .[16]

Burton's escape to the East had been tempered by acute inner contradictions. Like most eminent Victorians, he was representative of his era in some aspects, whilst being at serious odds with it in other aspects. His personality clearly exhibited his dual nature; he despised the London drawing-rooms, yet became crestfallen when his presence in them was no longer coveted as his notoriety increased and his career prospects dwindled. He conducted himself outrageously in society, while simultaneously hankering for a successful diplomatic career. He had a sexual curiosity that pushed him to research the penchants and perversions of various races while he lived quite tamely within the confines of a very prudish Victorian marriage. He found in the East an appeasement of his unconciliatory wants; the official who craved power was satisfied, as was the non-conformist adventurer who wished to discover the unknown. When Burton's wanderings in exotic lands had been curtailed by the Foreign Office, who exiled him to Trieste as consul, he wrote to Monckton Milnes complaining that the tame surroundings had little to stimulate his penchant for the bizarre or his love of danger:

> And now I'm sick of it. I want to be up and doing. Central Asia or Central Africa or something of the kind. I have applied for Tiflis. One of the clerks says 'Between us two they are going to appoint a military man who has something of the language.' I replied I *am* a military man who knows something of the language. *Au diable!*[17]

And as he described himself, he *was* the man trained in the

Empire's army, learned in the languages of its colonies, and able to represent its imperialistic beliefs. Perhaps he reproduced those beliefs in too startling a manner, and in a mild way, had to be punished for such transgression. Because he represented the age's fantasies so fully and so openly he represented at the same time a threat to cautious and secretive officialdom. The scholar in Burton (like the scholar in Galland) despised his audience's taste for the erotic texts he continued to 'translate'; surprised at the enthusiastic reception accorded his *Arabian Nights*, he wrote with embittered irony: 'I translate a doubtful book in my old age, and I immediately make sixteen thousand guineas. Now that I know the tastes of England we need never be without money.'[18] But the accepted and acceptable texts were too tenacious to be dismantled, and even Burton's erudition ultimately gave way to them. He catered to the prevalent taste while at the same time despising it. He could not break out of the discourse that engulfed nineteenth-century travel.

A BLUNT REPRISAL

One Victorian traveller in particular stands out for having championed the East. This was Wilfrid Scawen Blunt, who preferred to side with the colonised against his colonising compatriots. He espoused their struggles for liberty in a manner reminiscent of Lord Byron (whose grand-daughter he had married), writing eloquently in defense of their national causes.

A son of the landed gentry, Blunt was embued with an affinity for the pastoral, which led him to entertain sympathetic feelings for those associated with the countryside. The Arabs he considered still representative of the pastoral and chivalric tradition which was being quickly eroded by Victorian industrialism and its new money. They were noble, generous, proud, and, in their full robes on their fine horses,[19] they were picturesque as well. On one of his early voyages, when travelling in French North Africa, Blunt was struck by the contrast between Arabs and French colonists. He wrote:

The contrast between their noble pastoral life on the one hand, with their camel herds and horses, a life of high tradition filled with the memory of heroic deeds, and on the other hand the ignoble squalor of the Frank settlers, with their wineshops and their swine, was one which could not escape us, or fail to rouse in us an angry sense of the incongruity which has made of these last the lords of the land and of those their servants.[20]

This trip to Algeria awakened in the young traveller a sympathy which was to prove lasting for the colonised. At the time, however, as he confessed in retrospect, it remained a naive kind of sympathy with no political dimension to it.

It was India that changed matters for Blunt, providing as it did a stark example of Western misrule in the East. It was there, on surveying the impoverished and terrified peasants, that Blunt came to his conclusions about the true nature of European colonisation. He wrote home angrily about the Salt Tax, which the British authorities had imposed and which they used violence to enforce.[21] To those imperialist apologists who argued that the British were in India in order to develop it, Blunt had only this to say: '. . . if we go on developing the country at the present rate the inhabitants will have, sooner or later, to resort to cannibalism, for there will be nothing but each other left to eat.'[22] Blunt described the famine that had stricken the Indian countryside, attributing it in great part to the mismanagement of the country under British rule.[23] He noted the breaches of justice prevalent then, and advocated self-government for the Indians as the only solution for an intolerable situation: 'What India really asks for as the goal of her ambitions is self-government – that is to say, that not merely executive but legislative and financial power should be vested in the native hands.'[24] Blunt, however, despite his excellent intentions, was unable to make the final commitment to Indian independence in matters military; he continued to regard as a necessity an English military presence there.[25] But to give Blunt his due, he concedes that in this he expressed his own opinion only, and 'that native opinion is in favour of native military service'.[26]

Unlike the greater majority of his compatriots, Blunt was sympathetic to Islam and admired and respected it as a noble religion. Writing of his book, *The Future of Islam*, he said:

In it I committed myself without reserve to the Cause of Islam as essentially the 'Cause of Good' over an immense portion of the world, and to be encouraged, not repressed, by all who cared for the welfare of mankind.[27]

His sympathy for Islam would eventually lead him to champion the Arab cause against European intervention and Ottoman injustice. As such a champion, he foreshadowed the career of T. E. Lawrence, whose mentor in many ways he was. However, Blunt was capable of a more generous attitude towards the Arabs than Lawrence ever was; in fact, he respected them as equals, as fellow aristocrats, as 'gentlemen of the desert'.[28] Unlike Burton, Doughty and Lawrence, Blunt would never deviate from this initial and sympathetic assessment of Bedouin qualities. He continued to admire their profound religious piety and their egalitarian vision of society, where ruling sheikhs accepted with ease the respect that was their due as men of high birth, but indulged in no vulgar show of pomp or power. Indeed, with time, Blunt came to identify more and more closely the Arab sheikh with the English squire. His sympathy for the Arabs was, to a great extent, dependent on his own belief in aristocratic supremacy, and unfortunately, on his hostility to the Jews.

After an extended trip to Nejd, Blunt came away with the conviction that in order to regenerate the enlightened life of the desert and tap the Arabs' full potential, they must first be freed from the yoke of Ottoman rule.[29] It was with this conviction that he concocted wild schemes for moving the Caliphate from Constantinople to Meccah. This move was to be carried out under the benign protection of the British government, who, as Blunt chose to believe, had inherited a long tradition of tolerance to Islam, a tradition that was lacking in other European nations. The gentlemen at the Foreign Office to whom Blunt communicated his plan did not share his enthusiasm. It would take a few decades for them to realise the expediency of Blunt's strategy. By then, his plans would be carried out, with no glory for him, by his devoted disciple, 'Lawrence of Arabia'. Blunt's heartfelt if naive vision of Arab rebirth would be twisted into a political trap that would ultimately serve imperialist ends, a consequence of no small irony for a man who died a vehement anti-imperialist.

When Blunt's hopes for Arab nationalism in Arabia were dashed by the political climate of the times, and after a visit to

Egypt where he encountered the leader of the army's revolt against the despotic Khedive Tawfiq, Ahmad Arabi, Blunt decided to take up his pen as fervent apologist for the Egyptian Nationalists. He described his deepening acquaintance with Arabi in his book, *The Secret History of the English Occupation of Egypt*, writing on the morning of his departure from Cairo:

> I paid a last visit to Arabi the morning of the day I left for England, 27th February. I had been little more than three months in Egypt, and it seemed to me like a lifetime, so absorbing had been the interests they had brought me. I looked upon Egypt already like a second *patria*, and intended to throw in my lot with the Egyptians as if they were my own countrymen.[30]

However, constitutional reform without bloodshed soon proved mere wishful thinking, for the French and the English, nervous about their investment in the Khedive's corrupt autocracy, decided to crush the popular uprising once and for all. The Anglo-French Joint Note and the indiscriminate bombing of Alexandria led to Arabi's defeat in September 1882 by Wolseley's forces. Blunt could no longer salvage the damage done by his country to the Egyptian national cause; using his influence and his private fortune, he was able to have the death sentence on Arabi and his followers lightened to life exile in Ceylon. This whole episode had not only been a historic tragedy – as far as Blunt was concerned, it was a personal defeat as well, and one that left him embittered and angry.

But it would not be the last time Blunt took up his pen to write for Egypt. He soon published the important *Atrocities of Justice under British Rule in Egypt*, in which he uncovered the crimes committed under Lord Cromer's government of that country. Blunt's stated object was

> to show the essentially inequitable basis on which criminal relations between Englishman and native, especially between English officer and Egyptian fellah, have been made to stand, as often as it has been thought advisable on political grounds to uphold the former and punish the latter.[31]

Blunt described in detail several cases in which innocent victims died for nothing. The most brutal of these was the Denshawai case, which stirred a great deal of controversy both in Egypt and in Europe.

The particulars of the case were as follows. Five English officers camped on a site in the Egyptian countryside, and commenced shooting pigeons at a village called Denshawai. They soon wounded four villagers who sought to refrain them from further shooting of the domesticated pigeons which constituted the village's main livelihood. A fight soon ensued when they remained adamant, and they were wounded by some villagers who surrounded them. One of the English officers, a Captain Bull, overcome by his attempt at flight, died from concussion of the brain and sunstroke.[32] A villager attempted to save him but failed. English soldiers soon arrived on the scene, and seeing the same villager who was tending Captain Bull, they fell on him immediately and murdered him with the butt-ends of their rifles, assuming him to be the killer. Lord Cromer then sent an English official advisor to the village, who arrested five bystanders and instantly requested the death sentence. A mock-trial was held a few days later, but as Blunt points out, the ordering of the gallows took place before the trial ever began.[33]

When the trial did take place, it consisted of a very partial jury consisting (in a jury of five) of three Englishmen, one of whom was an officer, one a Christian Egyptian noted for his close ties to the local British authorities, and one a Muslim Egyptian. When that latter expressed his realisation that the English were the guilty party, he was severely rebuked by the English judge, who told him: 'Your contradiction nowise astonishes me. All Egyptians are alike. Not one to be trusted.'[34]

One of the English officers involved in the incident, the curiously-named Major Pine Coffin, gave false witness; he testified that the pigeons he and his party had been shooting were wild ones, and therefore public property. He was thereby acquitted of all charges.

The accused Egyptians, on the other hand, were hounded together like animals and given scarcely a chance. They had no defence at all – the outcome was prearranged and inevitable:

Of the fifty-seven accused fifty are caged within barred enclosures. The seven others have disappeared and will be judged *en contumace*. The interrogatory of these fifty-seven accused lasted exactly thirty minutes, that is to say they gave them no time at all to defend themselves.[35]

Almost as soon as the sham trial ended the hangings began. Blunt describes in detail the ascent to the gallows of the first man, one of the village elders, condemned to death in order to make an example of him before his village. Blunt writes:

> The mudir gives the order summoning the first of the condemned, an old man of seventy, still hale, with white beard, who comes out of the tent without making a false step over the clods of earth which he treads down barefooted.
>
> Brought along between two soldiers with fixed bayonets, he listens to the sentence of death read out, his countenance untroubled; with a firm step he walks to the scaffold and with equal steadiness mounts the steps. He places himself beneath the gallows opposite the village where for three quarters of a century his life has passed in peace; he must recognize his wife, his children, his relations, who cry loudly while stretching out their arms to him.[36]

The Denshawai incident provided an illustrative example of how 'justice' was meted out to the local population in Egypt under colonial rule. It was yet another instance that dispelled the myth of a free Egypt under British 'protection'; Britain was there by force, and entirely for her own ends. Blunt uncovers several cases in which 'the English government was politically interested in the guilt of the accused being proved'.[37] It was a tactic in the strategy of colonisation: terrorise a population in order to rule over it. For instance, when Professor Palmer (who was sent on a secret political mission to the bedouins) was killed while crossing the desert, there was a great uproar among the British public and many British officials, of whom Burton was one, cried for very severe punitive measures that would set an example among the tribes. Colonel Warren saw to it that such measures were implemented, and five innocent men were hanged, and many women and children imprisoned.[38] It was Kitchener revenging Gordon, albeit on a much smaller, and less conspicuously-brutal scale. Martial law was enforced in Egypt in order to give the British freer rein in administering 'justice':

It is not too much to say that under the Decree of 1895 a native Egyptian could be legally sentenced to death, even death by impalement or crucifixion, for having by a blow prevented or resented the violation of his wife by an English soldier.[39]

Blunt was perhaps the only Victorian traveller to challenge the notions of Empire with such passionate conviction, and with such consistency. The majority of travellers were content to bow to imperialist logic if they did not whole-heartedly support the imperial foundation. Some travellers were ironic observers of the world beyond the seas, and of their own compatriots' attitudes towards it, but they rarely succeeded in neutralising established views by merely mocking them.

Albert Smith, for instance, was one traveller who held the majority of travelogues in a good deal of suspicion. He saw through the classic wiles used to distort or embellish the subject at hand by traditional writers of Orientalist accounts. He referred to this quite common phenomenon in the Preface to the Second Edition of his book, *A Month at Constantinople*:

The absurdly false and over-coloured medium through which the majority of travellers have hitherto thought it essential to view the East will, I hope, soon be broken down. I have done my best to throw a stone at it.[40]

Smith's critical stance, however, was not at all a political one as Blunt's would be. His main quarrel with traditional portrayals of the East was one with tone rather than content. He disliked the sugary and florid manner used by numerous travellers to describe a romanticised reality. He judged such descriptions to be guilty of falsely raising a reader's expectations; the sights of Constantinople, for example, 'had been so ridiculously written up, and overpraised, that expectation could not possibly be gratified'.[41] Smith's own literary strategy, on the other hand, was to take the wind out of the elegant or sentimental notions that a reader might have of a place by giving him a segment of unredeemed (and absurd) 'reality' instead. His was an attempt to demystify the East by using a certain *tone* in his descriptions of it: but there was no serious endeavour to understand or to appreciate what he saw. Indeed, there was hardly anything of the serious in the strain he pursued in his travelogue; he merely debunked the pomposity of previous travelogues without truly differing in essence from their givens.

In style, Smith is a modernist because of the 'cool' quality of his narrative. His casualness, however, is not without its prejudice, and his focus seems ultimately to be both narrow and exclusive. His sympathy with what he sees is noticeably limited; indeed, he has very little patience with a great many things. The humour with which he describes the sights of Constantinople often verges on the childish. Entering the mosque at St Sophia, he perceived the persons at prayer in a ridiculous light, as they 'were constantly bobbing up and down, touching the ground with their foreheads, and springing up again on their heels, in a ludicrous fashion'.[42] When he saw a group of whirling dervishes performing their spiritual dance, Smith reacted in the following manner: 'There was something inexpressibly sly and offensive in the appearance of these men, and the desire one felt to hit them hard in the face became uncomfortably dominant.'[43]

Indeed, one is left with the impression that Smith was a 'Muscular Christian' in the literal sense of the word. He has very little time for Islam, and his expression of his impatience often verges on the medieval. The Turk, he says, clings 'to his religion and his Koran: that will always endure, for the wily impostor who drew up the Mohammedan code so flattered the passions of his followers, that their allegiance was certain as long as human nature remained unchanging'.[44] Here again are the early conventions of Christian polemic: Muhammad as Impostor, Islam as a creed that catered to the base senses.

Even the traditional expectations that a Western reader entertains and usually finds gratified in the East are not so in Smith's case. The Seraglio leaves him cold, not having enough of the 'oriental' about it.[45] The Odalisques of the imagination, the Sultan's favourites, the Scheherazades of Western lore, are nowhere to be seen. Instead, Smith perceives only plainness and ugliness. Of Turkish women he has this to say:

> Their complexions are pallid and unhealthy-looking, which may, in some measure, result from want of legitimate exercise; and they become prematurely aged. There is not, I imagine, a more perfect representation of a witch to be found, than an old Turkish woman affords, when seen hobbling, with a long staff, along the dingy alleys of Constantinople.[46]

A pragmatic man who prides himself on his ability to call a spade a spade, who delights in sneering gleefully at readers' illusions, Smith is nevertheless irked when one of his own expectations of Oriental splendour bites the dust as he watches a simply-dressed Sultan arrive at the mosque to pray:

> A dream of the Arabian Nights had been somewhat harshly dispelled. I had seen a Sultan – a great monarch, holding as high a rank as the father of Aladdin's Princess Badroulbadour – and but for his fez, he might have passed for a simple foreign gentleman from Leicester Square.[47]

Thus, Smith leaves Constantinople after a month with few Orientalist illusions, but with little affection for it, with its incessantly barking dogs, its very active bedbugs, its inactive and plain women, its ludicrous dervishes and lustreless seraglio. Smith's is an entertaining if superficial travel account, without the self-glorifying note that jars in the narratives of less down-to-earth travellers. Smith did not strike any of the aggravating poses that many of his compatriots did, but was content to present himself to his audience as a quick-witted if sharp-tongued Cockney, out for a good laugh on the Bosphorus. His narrative was as unpretentious as his name, and it shared little in the self-importance intrinsic to the bulk of English travel narrative about the East.

PILGRIMS' PROGRESS

One strong motive that prompted Englishmen to make the journey East was religion. It was the need to seek out the roots of a Christianity that had come to be threatened by new materialism and scientific discovery. Lyell and Darwin had undermined to a great extent the established religious beliefs, and works such as Strauss's *Leben Jesu* (1836) and Renan's *La Vie de Jésus* (1863) had encouraged a more secular approach to the study of Scriptures. The old orthodoxy was foundering under the onslaught of such startling and unsettling revelations; piety had come to be in danger. By the second half of the century, however, a religious restitution began gaining ground. 'Pilgrimages' came to be relevant once more, as pilgrims sought out Biblical illustration that would help confirm their faith. There were 'Holy Land

Excursions', arranged by Thomas Cook, to facilitate such pilgrimage; these created a touristic buffer zone that prevented the traveller from undergoing discomfort, and simulated his religious sensibilities at the same time. For the hardier travellers there was Arabia, which Thomas Cook did not include on his tours.

Among these pilgrims, Charles Doughty was the most fervent and fanatical, eyeing his surroundings for all they could yield of Biblical significance. At every turn, the East recalls to his mind the Scriptures. A childless wife encountered in one of the Bedouin settlements is likened to Sarah, the darkness of bedouin skin recalls the maiden's pigments in the Song of Solomon, and forms of oath exchange are reminiscent of 'words we hear from gentle Jonah's mouth, in his covenant with the climbing David'.[48]

Doughty's decision to journey through Arabia had initially been sparked by his desire to decipher inscriptions on the ruins of Medain Salih, which he suspected had Scriptural significance. He notes in the Preface to the second edition of *Arabia Deserta* that his strong interest in Biblical research had induced him to risk the hazard of visiting them. His more general religious motive for undertaking such a journey is summed up when he writes:

> As for the nomad Arabs . . . we may see in them that desert life, which was followed by their ancestors, in the Biblical tents of Kedar. While the like phrases of their nearly-allied and not less ancient speech, are sounding in our ears, and their like customs, come down from antiquity, are continued before our eyes; we almost feel ourselves carried back to the days of the nomad Hebrew Patriarchs . . . And we are better able to read the bulk of the Old Testament books, with that further insight and understanding, which comes of a living experience.[49]

This 'living experience', when found to have ties with a past that figured in Christian tradition, was deemed positive and noteworthy; but if the beliefs and customs of the indigenous population differed from what the European observer desired them to be like, and if they possessed a connotative value other than dramatic re-enactment of Bible scenes, then they were rejected because they disturbed the static image and the pre-conceived idea. Doughty's rejection in particular borders on what seems an archaic fanaticism when compared with the more subtle intolerance of his contemporaries. He lapses into Crusader language to convey his Crusader's intolerance:

> Are not Mohammed's saws to-day the mother belief of a tenth part of mankind? What had the world been? if the tongue had not wagged, of this fatal Ishmaelite! Even a thin-witted religion that can array an human multitude, is a main power in the history of the unjust world. Perilous every bond which can unite many of the human millions, for living and dying! Islam and the commonwealth of the Jews are as great secret conspiracies, friends only of themselves and to all without of crude iniquitous heart, unfaithful, implacable. But the pre-Islamic idolatrous religion of the kaaba was cause that the soon ripe Mawmetry rotted not soon again.[50]

Doughty's sense of religious superiority was typical of his Age's, which saw itself as propagating the only system of belief that was correct and could enlighten (as in Napoleon's laicised version, the *mission civilisatrice*) those less fortunate. In a study of European rivalry with the Orient, *Islam, Europe and Empire*, Norman Daniel elaborated on this particular conviction of religious superiority, writing:

> The new conviction of superiority arose from technologies and techniques of government, but it took the form of a belief in Christian superiority ... Superiority was explained as the result, not of new techniques, but of old morality: often, as though the Christian morality had been necessary to achieve the techniques. There was revived in the Victorian Age the religious and moral fervour of the Middle Ages, speaking with the modern accent of material progress.[51]

Doughty's sense of religious superiority was linked to his contempt for Islam. He resented the fact that Arabia (which he would have liked to be an illustration of Biblical lore, and only that) was peopled by inhabitants who claimed a distinct heritage from Christian Europe's. His religious hostility runs like a thread throughout his narrative. His language, most often angry, sometimes verges on the abusive:

> I wondered with a secret horror at the fiend-like malice of these

fanatical Bedouins, with whom no keeping in touch nor truth of honourable life, no performance of good offices, might win the least favour from the dreary, inhuman, and for our sins, inveterate dotage of their blood-guilty religion.[52]

Doughty abhorred Islam the religion as he abhorred its live, concrete manifestations. When in the course of his journey he meets an Italian traveller who had read the Qur'an sympathetically, Doughty launches forth indignantly, plainly noting his own contempt for that book and for its sympathisers – most especially if they happened to be misguided Europeans:

> I said I could never find better than a headache in the farrago of the Koran; and it amazed me that one born in the Roman country, and under the name of Christ, should waive these prerogatives, to become the brother of Asiatic barbarians.[53]

Thus, being a Christian and being a European were two prerogatives that no man in his right mind should willingly waive. For they set him above the encountered native, the fanatical bedouin, the 'Asiatic barbarian'.

Like Lane, Doughty had turned to the East for a temporary career. A solitary man, grudgeful and carping, he felt happiest when observing glaciers off the Norwegian coast, or when walking endlessly though Cambridgeshire fens. He found Arabia's desert to his liking (although its inhabitants stirred his most ignoble passions). It was a haven from the English country society he had been born to but felt helplessly shy in. It gave him a more satisfying personality to inhabit, one that he could cast from him once it had met the need that engendered it.

Doughty liked to perceive himself as a Christian Patriarch, moving through Arabia with Biblical stature. Thus, he was preoccupied with *sounding* like a Christian Patriarch; he recounted his journey in a style that strongly resembled that of the Scriptures. He wished to give his narrative epic proportions. He had also set himself the task of refurbishing the English language with the linguistic splendour he was convinced it had lost. In his introductory pages he informs his reader that he was 'a disciple of the divine Muse of Spencer and Venerable Chaucer'.[54] But such a self-conscious stance led him to choose a stilted and archaic vocabulary, which produced a narrative as cumbrous and inelegant as a trip on camel-back.

Ironically enough, Doughty's English came to sound 'foreign'. Nevertheless, its archaicisms came to be considered by traditional Orientalists as befitting an account of an archaic people. The critic A. J. Arberry, for instance, thought Doughty's 'tense, nervous, patriarchal prose' betrayed countless traces of a 'mind that thought in Arabic'.[55] Why archaic English should betray an Arabic-thinking mind is not altogether clear; but what becomes obvious from reading *Arabia Deserta* is that in returning to such heavy archaicisms, Doughty succeeded only in transmitting sedimented forms. Doughty's language served as an alienating device which distanced the people it described from his readers. It exiled them to a spurious ancientness where they were no longer recognisable as contemporary beings with similar wants and aspirations. Here are some passages in which he describes bedouin life in this artificial manner. The first is a description of women at their tasks and children tending sheep:

> Children drive their little weanling troops to the next bushes and the valley sides. The hareem take up their spinning: of other housewifery they go now nearly empty-handed; there is no butter-making nor daily milking. There is not a handmill heard any more in the menzil; they have no more ado to fetch water.[56]

Here is a description of a bedouin wife in which Doughty seeks to evoke the atmosphere of the Song of Solomon: 'Tall was this fair young wife and freshly clad as a beloved; her middle small girt with a gay scarlet lace: barefoot she went upon the waste sand with a beautiful erect confidence of the hinds.'[57] Doughty often created new words in English in imitation of Arabic ones, or he inserted expressions in Arabic into his narrative or translated Arabic turns of phrase into English in order to achieve the desired quaint effect.

> At a cross street there met us two young gallants. 'Ha! said one of them to Aly, this stranger with thee is a Nasrâny;'—and turning to me, the coxcombs bid me, 'Good morrow, khawaja': I answered them, 'I am no khawaja, but an Engleysy; and how am I of your acquaintance?'—'Last night we had word of your

coming from Boreyda: Aly, whither goest thou with him?' That
poor man, who began to be amazed, hearing his guest named
Nasrâny, answered, 'To Zâmil.'—'Zâmil is not yet sitting; then
bring the Nasrâny to drink coffee at my beyt.'[58]

Such passages made *Arabia Deserta* a receptacle for all traditional
stereotypes of the bedouins: they were religious fanatics, liars,
thieves. Doughty had very little sympathy for them. Even
Bedouin generosity – the one positive trait that Europe allowed
the Arabs – he claimed was capricious at best, even though he
sponged off of it for over a year. He portrayed the Arabs as
superstitious beings who lived in filth while cloaked in holiness.
One much-quoted phrase sums up his mental picture of the
Arabs: 'The Semites are like to a man sitting in a cloaca to the
eyes, and whose brows touch heaven.'[59] Why the metaphor of a
man sitting in excrement with his brows touching heaven sums up
the Arab's strengths and weakness is disturbingly ambiguous.
Indeed, only a mind on hostile terms with what it was describing
could summon up such an image, and only a reader of a similarly
hostile disposition could find such an image appropriate. T. E.
Lawrence was exactly such a reader, a disciple of Doughty's in
alienation from the East. In introducing the third edition of *Arabia
Deserta*, Lawrence wrote:

> The realism of the book is complete. Doughty tries to tell the full
> and exact truth of all that he saw . . . His picture of the Semites,
> sitting to the eyes in a cloaca, but with their brows touching
> Heaven, sums up in full measure their strength and weakness,
> and the strange contradictions of their thought which quicken
> our curiosity at our first meeting them.[60]

What becomes clear in reading Lawrence on Doughty is the
similarity in language and perception in both of their narratives.
Perhaps it is such complicity of sentiment that led Lawrence to
lionise Doughty, and Doughty to feel genuine attachment to
Lawrence. The tone of *Arabia Deserta* is recreated in Lawrence's
Introduction to it, where he expresses the same vision of the
Semites:

> Semites have no half-tones in their register of vision . . . They do
> not understand our metaphysical difficulties, our self-
> questionings.

Semites are black and white not only in vision, but in their inner furnishing. They are a limited narrow-minded people whose inert intelligence lies incuriously fallow . . . They show no longing for great industry, no organisations of mind or body anywhere.[61]

Not surprisingly, Lawrence considered Doughty's tome a bible of its kind. He believed it to be 'one of the great prose works of literature'.[62] In a highly imprecise observation, Lawrence wrote that Doughty had moved among the Arabs dispassionately. Every page of *Arabia Deserta* refutes this claim. Doughty's language is charged throughout with passion; with hostility, scorn, loathing, and in rare instances of truce, with grudging fascination.

Lawrence also claimed that Doughty had maintained a 'perfect judgement', since he managed to be an Arab in dress and a European in mind – a duality Lawrence himself would emulate. But despite their show of superficial integration, both Doughty and Lawrence remained rigidly outside the culture they wrote of. Doughty wrote that the sun had made him an Arab, but had never warped him to Orientalism. He was made an Arab momentarily, by the dress that he adopted and the effect of a climate that slightly darkened his white skin. But he continued a stranger in the bedouin booths precisely because he chose to remain one. He could not even feel the paternalistic (and contemptuous) sympathy of the Orientalist for the Arabs. He remained conspicuously outside both realms, moving sulkily along in order to arrive at last, as the final line of his book records, 'to the open hospitality of the British Consulate'.[63]

Since the Englishman in the East depended on the wholeness of his identity remaining intact, any threat to its intactness plunged him into a chaos that overwhelmed him. He had to remind himself continually that he was different (and superior) to the community he placed himself in temporarily. He could have no real commerce with its members. Like Doughty, Lawrence could never really see 'through the veil at once of two customs, two educations, two environments'. He felt no deep understanding of the Arabs; they served only as a means of self-glorification. He had always seen himself, under the influence of the romantic readings of his adolescence, beyond which he never truly progressed, as a figure who could lead and inspire. But despite having chosen the Arabs as the people he would lead, he felt no real sympathy for them or solidarity with their ideals. 'I was tired to death of these Arabs', he wrote, 'petty incarnate Semites'. He spoke of the alien and primitive functioning of their minds: 'Their thoughts were at ease only in extremes. They pursued the logic of several incompatible opinions to absurd ends, without perceiving the incongruity.'[64] Lawrence insisted on the primitiveness of the Arabs' mental functioning: 'The Arab mind', he wrote, is 'strange and dark, full of depressions and exaltations, lacking in rule'.[65]

Lawrence may have felt the contagion of such lack of rule as he imagined thrived among the Arabs, as his chaotic and emotive narrative often points to. His writings were suspect in content and written to stir up emotions that do not correspond to the events described. But they proved invaluable to the manufacture of a hero, of a sentimental myth. The 'Lawrence of Arabia' fabrication kept the man from real scrutiny; it hid his weaknesses, his unreliability, and exaggerated what positive traits he possessed way beyond recognition. Sometimes, the real Lawrence dared to look beyond the myth which he himself had manufactured, and in those thoughtful hours when he pondered the duality of his persona, he also remarked the precise motives for his country's flirtation with the bedouin tribes. In hours such as these he could be honest about the deception he was helping to perpetuate:

> . . . not being a perfect fool, I could see that, if we won the war, the promises to the Arabs were dead paper. Had I been an honourable adviser I would have sent my men home, and not let them risk their lives for such stuff.[66]

But honourable action was out of the question if it meant siding against one's own government for the sake of a native people. And if men like Lawrence felt, in weary hours, certain qualms about their roles, these were hardly ever serious misgivings with long-term effects. Lawrence had described his own feeling about his affiliation with the bedouins in the following words: 'My own ambition is that the Arabs should be our first brown dominion.'[67] He was a new-fangled imperialist, disguised in the flowing robes of the native, intent on sublimating his motives and mesmerising his audience.

Lawrence's 'heroic' epic begins with a passage that seems at strange odds with the lofty title. It describes the homosexual relations that Lawrence claimed took place all around him in the desert:

> Friends quivering together in the yielding sand with intimate hot limbs in supreme embrace, found there hidden in the darkness a sensual co-efficient of the mental passion which was welding our souls and spirits in one flaming effort. Several, thirsting to punish appetites they could not wholly prevent, took a savage pride in degrading the body, and offered themselves fiercely in any habit which promised physical pain or filth.[68]

What this unlikely description of quivering bedouins was supposed to achieve is unclear. Perhaps it was Lawrence's subconscious portrayal of his own repressed desires. For like André Gide, he sought in the East that sexual 'liberation' that the Frenchman had found in North Africa with Tunisian fisherboys whose services he paid for. Lawrence's love for Dahoum marked him deeply; it has often been suggested that he dedicated *Seven Pillars of Wisdom* to him. The dedicatory poem reads as follows:

> I loved you, so I drew these tides
> of men into my hands and wrote my will
> across the sky in stars
>
> . . . Love the way-weary, groped to
> your body,
> our brief wage ours for the moment,
> Before earth's soft hand explored your shape,
> and the blind worms grew fat upon
> your substance.
>
> Men prayed that I set our work, the inviolate
> house, as a memory of you.[69]

Like the majority of English travellers to the East, Lawrence upheld the stereotypical image of the Easterner as sensualist. Whereas this supposed trait was described sympathetically in the case of the Arabs (who interested Lawrence), it was looked upon with horror in the case of the Turks (whom Lawrence hated). In describing his alleged 'rape' at Der'aa, Lawrence took the image of the sexually-obsessed Oriental – the Turkish garrison-commander, in this case – to its furthest and most ridiculous extreme: 'He began to fawn on me, saying how white and fresh I was, how fine my hands and feet, and how he would let me off drills and duties, make me his orderly, even pay me wages, if I would love him.'[70] As this description is of an incident that never truly took place,[71] the passage is of interest since it reflects Lawrence's private preoccupations. He chose to portray himself as the frail, fair victim at the mercy of a brutish Oriental, who would stop at nothing in order to win his favours.

The 'Lawrence of Arabia' hero appealed to a tendency in many Westerners towards hero-worship. It became a difficult myth to undermine, fulfilling as it did all the ideal attributes of the Englishman abroad. He was courageous (as was Lawrence, by his own account, in the desert), capable of enduring (and in this case, enjoying[72]) terrible tests of stamina, and the bodily wounds and mental degradation inflicted by (alleged) sexual assault and ensuing imprisonment. The Englishman had also to be mentally as well as physically superior to those he moved amongst, as we have seen. But such mythologising, so necessary to an imperialist world-view, produced myths that were merely apt reflections of the tormented selves who created them. Lawrence's narration, which expressed a turbulent inward journey, but which had little historical validity as document, was yet one more example of a Westerner's delusions of grandeur in the East.

5　'Among the Believers'

The journey embarked on, away from the familiar and into the universe's otherness, always contains elements that are problematic. In the hope of new vistas the traveller moves, while dreading as he approaches them their unknown features[He seeks 'exceptions, exclusions, incongruities, contradictions',[1] yet knows that if he encounters such divergences they will overpower him.] He must therefore find some method of surpassing and surviving the journey: he seeks to assimilate the most easily available model he has of a city before arriving in it, a model that will be his point of reference as he travels, and his talisman against confusion and contamination. Often if he is profoundly frightened or irretrievably biased (as early European travellers to the Orient were) he will see nothing but his own construct or his compatriots' creation in the places that he passes through. Yet this is the extreme case, and more often, the predisposition of the traveller is more elusive to trace as we can appreciate in contemporary travel literature.

The journey's narrative, that soliloquizing the author engages in which an audience overhears, is peculiar in that it remains circular[It moves away from the self, yet returns more deeply into it the further the narrator moves into the unknown.] It portrays the traveller more faithfully than it records the travels. It leads the reader back, unintentionally perhaps and despite itself, to the emblematic Ithaca that originally provided the desire to move away from it, as it would ultimately provide the need to return.

Italo Calvino's Marco Polo, who enthrals with his narrative a sedentary Kublai Khan desiring details of his vast dominions, realises that the more

> one was lost in unfamiliar quarters of distant cities, the more one understood the other cities he had crossed to arrive there; and he retraced the stages of his journey, and he came to know

the port from which he had set sail, and the familiar places of his
youth, and the surroundings of home . . .[2]

The listening Khan, after having heard the Venetian wanderer
describe to him inumerable cities, spelled out the circularity of the
narrative when he said:

> 'There is still one of which you never speak.'
> Marco Polo bowed his head.
> 'Venice,' the Khan said.
> Marco smiled. 'What else do you believe I have been talking to
> you about?'[3]

For Venice is implicit in the description of all other cities; it is not
merely a place, but a method of comparison, an education, a
system of belief, a literature and a mythology. The original city
forms the traveller, provides him with his vision, predicts his
reactions and produces his narrative. It guards him against
dissipation (for in dissipation lies danger – Gulliver becomes a
travesty when overpowered by the voyage; it unhinges his mind,
making him prefer horses to humans) but it limits his ability
to see.

In the course of reading travel narrative we have observed how
certain images, once codified in language, become static and final.
We have remarked how travellers depended on each other's
testimony in forging their narrative: the place became the place
they had read about, the natives functioned as the traveller
imagined they would do. It was a reductive method, but in critical
times of political crises (during the Crusades, for instance) it
served its narrator well.

To start this examination of contemporary travel narrative, it
would be instructive to study the writings of a traveller who forms
a link between the nineteenth-century narrator and his twentieth-
century counterpart. This is Wilfrid Thesiger, whose book,
Arabian Sands, continues in the tradition of Burton, Doughty and
Lawrence. It is interesting to note that he was appreciated by his
country exactly within that tradition: for his labours, he was
awarded the 'Burton Memorial Medal' from the Royal Asiatic
Society, and the 'Lawrence of Arabia Medal' from the Royal
Central Asian Society.

Thesiger introduces his work with the claim that he had not

intended to keep a record of his journey through Arabia, but the encouragement of others had prompted him to write a book about the subject almost a decade after he had returned from his journey.[4] The work then proved invaluable since it was a personal registration of memories among the bedouins, and a public service since it recorded the details of the Arabia he had passed through, one that had begun to disintegrate under the onslaught of machinery and with the encroachment of material wealth. Material improvement brought moral decay; the new desecrated the old. Thus the noble Arabia, a land that had continued to be as archaic as it had always been and was so well-loved by the British for its atemporal qualities which they wished to uphold, was disappearing, degenerating:

> If anyone goes there now looking for the life I led they will not find it, for technicians have been there since, prospecting for oil. Today the desert where I have travelled is scarred with the tracks of lorries and littered with discarded junk imported from Europe and America. But this material desecration is unimportant compared with the demoralization which has resulted among the Bedu themselves.[5]

Thus according to Thesiger the changing patterns of life in Arabia had brought about demoralisation, for they were killing an ancient tradition, rendering the traditional patterns of bedouin life obsolete. Towns rather than the desert were now centres of the new activity, and to these the bedouins went, diminished, no longer the free spirits of the desert, unable to make use any longer of 'the qualities which once gave them mastery'.[6] Thesiger's view is the classic European one: the Western traveller, coming from a milieu of comfort and knowing that he would soon be returning to it, could well afford to voice conservationist sentiments. The Arab, that 'sometime Noble Savage',[7] was picturesque in his environment. He was static as the world moved, pure of all corrupting influences, a purity that greatly endeared him to a Western eye so appreciative of symbolic heroes. Disraeli, for instance, had illustrated such an appreciation in his novel, *Tancred*, admiring as he did the Arabs' archaic virtues which he saw as a product of their racial insularity. 'The decay of race', he wrote, 'is an inevitable necessity unless it lives in deserts and never mixes blood.'[8] Such a perception tells the reader something about

Disraeli's views on race, but very little about the Arabs themselves. For they were used as symbols that expressed each traveller's longings, ones that could be diverted to channel whatever he wished to express. If he wished for racial purity, then they were racially pure. If he admired chivalry, then they were chivalrous. If he happened to loathe other religions, then they were fanatics who embodied the evils of religious heresy (a view that was sustained by Doughty, for one). And since the English admired asceticism and praised those who lived it, they appreciated the bedouins as symbols of the Puritan ethic of abstinence and self-denial. It was as illustrations of this fundamental ethos that they had to be protected, had to be allowed to remain in conditions that would leave them unaltered. For if the conditions altered, then the symbol was in danger of altering too, and that was a danger the English feared, one that Thesiger described so fully.

Thesiger's prose, especially that of his prologue, is embellished in a manner reminiscent of Doughty and of Lawrence (who, aptly enough, is quoted at its end). The themes important to English narrative about Arabia all reappear here: Arabia as a harsh land, an easeless existence, an ancient place with few remnants of its ancientness still apparent, and most importantly, an experience that marks the traveller deeply:

> No man can live this life and emerge unchanged. He will carry, however faint, the imprint of the desert, the brand which marks the nomad; and he will have within him the yearning to return, weak or insistent according to his nature. For this cruel land can cast a spell which no temperate clime can match.[9]

The charm of such a journey lay mainly in the occasion it afforded for heroic action. It was a place that could put all the traveller's mental and physical capacities to test (a test he himself had set up, and one which he would ultimately judge the results of). Thesiger wrote of 'the satisfaction which comes from hardship and the pleasure which springs from abstinence'.[10]

In the East, Thesiger found a spectacle that could excite and divert. As a young man in Sudan, still newly-emerged from Oxford, he found what the literature he had read had promised him:

This was the Africa which I had read about as a boy and which
I had despaired of finding in the Sudan when I first saw
Khartoum: the long line of naked porters winding across a plain
dotted with grazing antelope; my trackers slipping through the
dappled bush as we followed a herd of buffalo; the tense
excitement as we closed in upon a lion at bay; the reeking red
shambles as we cut up a fallen elephant, a blood-caked youth
grinning out from between the gaping ribs.[11]

In the well-charted cities of Africa Thesiger felt despondent. His
quest was for something more exhilarating: 'I wanted colour and
savagery, hardship and adventure.'[12] But soon even the
'savagery' Africa can provide appears limited and leaves him
dissatisfied. He began looking for a more demanding challenge.
For this reason, the 'Empty Quarter' of Arabia began to seem
more and more tempting to him. It was with precisely this same
sense of challenge that Burton had embarked upon his
'pilgrimage' to Meccah, spurred by the need to conquer fear, test
his disguise, and prove his ability as unprecedented traveller in
dangerous regions. And just as Burton had been spurred to such
adventure by the writings of Burkhardt, so Thesiger was
prompted to his journey by the writings of two compatriots who
had preceded him – T. E. Lawrence and Bertram Thomas:

When I was at Oxford I had read *Arabia Felix* in which Bertram
Thomas described his journey. The month which I had already
spent in Danakil country had given me some appreciation and
understanding of desert life, and Lawrence's *Revolt in the Desert*
had awakened my interest in the Arabs.[13]

Thesiger dressed in Arab clothes during his journey, occasionally
posing as a Syrian merchant. He describes his self-consciousness
at first donning the unfamiliar garb:

As this was the first time I had worn Arab dress I felt extremely
self-conscious. My shirt was new, white, and rather stiff, very
noticeable among the Bedu's dingy clothes. They were all small
men, and as I am six foot two I felt as conspicuous as a
lighthouse, and as different from them as one of the R.A.F.[14]

This change in the externals of personality, however, no longer possesses the calculating dimension it did when Burton or Lane indulged in it. For Thesiger, it is a convenience only; he knows he cannot look a very convincing Arab, but basks in the pleasure of play-acting. In that knowledge lies the difference in approach from the nineteenth-century travellers who, in disguising themselves, were convinced of the effective power of their disguise. That conviction was part of the aura of Empire, part of the 'superior Englishman' myth that they clung to so tenaciously. Although Thesiger is a more thoughtful traveller (being removed in time from the circumstances that produced a Burton or a Lawrence), he is nonetheless proud of the tradition left him by his predecessors. His reverence for Bertram Thomas who had travelled in Arabia before him was indivisible from his reverence for the whole of that inherited tradition. When he speaks of Thomas, he resembles Lawrence speaking of Doughty. Thesiger wrote:

> He was the first European to come among them and he won their respect by his good nature, generosity, and determination. They remembered him as a good travelling companion. When I went among exclusive tribesmen sixteen years after he had left them, I was welcomed because I belonged to the same tribe as Thomas. I had only met him twice, in Cairo during the war, and then only for a few minutes. I should have liked to meet him again before he died, to tell him how much I owed him.[15]

Thus the myths of heroic action continue because they continue to be upheld by the adventurers' compatriots. The legend is sustained, having become necessary as a source of cultural pride.

Thesiger's narrative picks up themes we have already encountered in the nineteenth-century travelogues. We have observed his stress on the ancientness of Arabia, his admiration for its uninterrupted tenor. Like the travellers of a previous century who had perceived it as an illustration of biblical lore, Thesiger responds to its 'hallowdness'. The poverty of Arabia is a redeeming quality in his eyes, for it makes the bedouin a holy people. The virtues they possess are described as being inextricably linked to their poverty (thus they must not be very deep virtues, if they change with any change in material circumstance). Therefore, any escape from social misery would be a loss of the admirable heritage, of ascetic virtues. Thesiger's description of dislocated bedouins guarding the oil wells is an image that encapsulates this particular kind of perception.

We have observed that Thesiger is a more thoughtful traveller than many of his predecessors, and he is so by weight of historic circumstance as well as by personal disposition. His sympathy for the travelling companions he chooses from among the bedouins is complete; no such sympathy could have been possible even for Lawrence, who had written only two decades earlier. But Thesiger is a much less tormented narrator than Lawrence ever was, and his encounter with the bedouins did not have the shattering emotional effect that a similar encounter produced in Lawrence. Thesiger is nevertheless aware that he cannot be completely at one with the Arabs, but feels there is a bond which binds them together stronger than the divisive attributes of religion and race. The passage in Thesiger which confirms such a feeling would have been completely out of character for Lawrence:

> I was happy in the company of these men who had chosen to come with me. I felt affection for them personally, and sympathy for their way of life. But though the easy equality of our relationship satisfied me, I did not delude myself that I could be one of them. They were Bedu and I was not; they were Muslims and I was a Christian. Nevertheless, I was their companion and an inviolable bond united us, as sacred as the bond between host and guest, transcending tribal and family loyalties. Because I was their companion on the road, they would fight in my defence even against their brothers and they would expect me to do the same.[16]

Another positive trait that the British observed in the bedouins was their hardiness, their capacity for the abstemious life. This reflected the British preoccupation with an ethic of renunciation. Looking at his resting companions, Thesiger says this of them:

> Even tonight, when they considered themselves well off, these men would sleep naked on the freezing sand, covered only with their flimsy loincloths. I thought, too, of the bitter wells in the furnace heat of summer, when, hour by reeling hour, they watered thirsty, thrusting camels, until at last the wells ran dry and importunate camels moaned for water which was not there. I thought how desperately hard were the lives of the Bedu in

this weary land, and how gallant and how enduring was their spirit.[17]

Thesiger also describes the bedouins' fear for their honour, their great desire to be respected and appreciated by their fellow tribesmen. This desire would sometimes lead to dramatic action that possessed a theatricality that pleased the Western observer. Thesiger relates one such action recounted him by Glubb, reverting thus to the inevitable sustaining tradition of previous travellers among the Arabs:

> Glubb once told me of a Bedu sheikh who was known as the 'Host of the Wolves', because whenever he heard a wolf howl round his tent he ordered his son to take a goat out in the desert, saying he would have no one call on him for dinner in vain.[18]

It was this sense of drama that excited the Western viewer among the bedouin tents. And if the dramatic spectacle could be linked to a vision that was erotically stimulating as well, then the traveller would indeed have arrived at the place of his quest. One particular passage in Thesiger resembles that nineteenth-century preoccupation with the sexual East. At an encampment of bedouins watering their camels, he saw a woman whose beauty added to the scene's picturesqueness:

> There was a lovely girl working with the others on the well. Her hair was braided, except where it was cut in a fringe across her forehead, and fell in a curtain of small plaits round her neck. She wore various silver ornaments and several necklaces, some of large cornelians, others of small white beads. Round her waist she had half a dozen silver chains, and above them her sleeveless blue tunic gaped open to show small firm breasts. She was very fair.[19]

The jewelled beauty makes her appearance in most travel narrative as we have seen, but it is a bit startling to encounter her here, in the midst of desert poverty, and so oblivious of her clothing that the narrator was able to catch sight of her breasts. The story is, however, recounted a decade after it took place, and perhaps in this lapse of time the erotic details of the apparition are augmented. An aid to the observant Thesiger's appreciation of the girl's beauty is the fairness of her skin, since such colouring brought her closer to Western standards of beauty (as it did the 'Circassians' of Orientalist painting, as we have seen).

But Thesiger, though not indifferent to Eastern female attractiveness, was, like Gide and Lawrence, susceptible to the charms of Eastern boys. When a handsome Arab youth joins them in one of their encampments, Thesiger reacts in the following manner to the literary quality of the image before him:

> This boy had dressed only in a length of blue cloth, which he wore wrapped round his waist with one tasseled end thrown over his right shoulder, and his dark hair fell like a mane about his shoulders. He had a face of classic beauty, pensive and rather sad in repose, but which lit up when he smiled, like a pool touched by the sun. Antinous must have looked like this, I thought, when Hadrian first saw him in the Phrygian woods. The boy moved with effortless grace, walking as women walk who have carried vessels on their heads since childhood. A stranger might have thought that his smooth pliant body would never bear the rigours of desert life, but I knew how deceptively enduring were these Bedu boys who looked like girls.[20]

The passage contains a great many nineteenth-century themes: the concentration on the boy's beauty would have appealed to a Victorian reader, tightly trapped as he was in his confining apparel and social codes. And the boy is described as being no mere savage: he is placed within a tradition of beauty that is Classical. The Hellenistic reference refines what would have otherwise been mere physical attraction and elevates it into something more precious (In this same manner, Oscar Wilde had compared his love for Alfred Douglas to the Greek tradition of homosexual love in the letter that was to lead to his downfall when used against him in the courtsuit). Thesiger sublimates any desire for the boy into a purely literary attraction: his mind leaps to Greek literature in order to borrow a metaphor that would strike a responsive chord in his reader.

The boy described possesses a body like a girl's, thus evoking a double-edged sensuality: he is boy and girl at once, having the traditional fragility of the female with the traditional strength of the male. Thesiger soon reveals that this slight figure is the best hunter in the tribe.

Like Burton and Doughty, Thesiger posed, while among the Arabs, as a man of medicine. In the sequel to *Arabian Sands*, his book, *The Marsh Arabs*, Thesiger takes the tradition of 'doctoring' the natives to its extreme when he circumcises young Arab boys in the encampments he passes through. And to aid the voyeuristic fantasy of such intimacy if it should lag, he provides the reader with several photographic impressions of the doctored boys.[21] Faced with such images, one wonders how far such documentation has moved away from the tropes of Orientalist painting. It would seem that the documentary absurdity of the travelogue can know no bounds, and can hardly alter at all.

The next two travellers we will examine, Canetti and Naipaul, are less straightforward examples of this tradition of travel writing, but do nevertheless fit neatly into it. They are outsiders to it by birth, but strongly linked to it by education and acquired culture. This points to the fact that travel narrative does not depend so much on the traveller's individual gaze as it does on the education he has received, the myths he for particular reasons cherishes, and the political and social structures he belongs to or functions within.

Elias Canetti's *The Voices of Marrakesh* is his account of a journey to that Moroccan city, or rather, his recreation of that experience (he is writing *fiction*; the non-fiction genre of the travelogue is a creative convention only). Canetti is first and foremost on a journey through a host of startling images. He offers the reader a passage into an Orient that is pure *tableau vivant* in the manner of Flaubert. There is never any deeper entrance beyond the series of queer images into Marrakesh as a complex reality. Canetti's Orient, though described with a compassion which was lacking in nineteenth-century descriptions, is still a classically static one. All the conventional themes surface in it, as if they provide the only keys to the understanding of the new landscape.

Canetti's Morocco is exotic in the special nineteenth-century sense of the term (that is, barbaric, different, other). It is attractive precisely because it remains incomprehensible; it cannot be defined clearly, and therefore offers mystery to spell relief from the boredom of daily existence. Segalen's essay on notions of the exotic had put it thus:

Définition du prefixe *Exo* dans sa plus grande généralisation possible. Tout ce qui est 'en dehors' de l'ensemble de nos faits de conscience actuels, quotidiens, tout ce qui n'est pas notre 'tonalité mentale' coutumiere.[22]

Canetti's journey is a voyage into all that is bizarre and horrific, with only tenuous ties to external reality.

Canetti begins his narrative with the mention of camels (the obvious beast traditionally associated with the East, and the one most conspicuous to the Western gaze). 'I came into contact with camels on three occasions', he begins, 'and each occasion ended tragically.'[23] This sentence sets the tone for Canetti's whole encounter with the East, which will also have tragic connotations. His first encounter with camels is at the camel market, deserted when he arrives there but for one shrieking beast, rabid and lame, being dragged to the slaughterhouse. This image continues to pursue him after he and his companion leave the scene. It becomes a recurring motif in the narrative:

> We often spoke of the rabid camel during the next few days; its despairing movements had made a deep impression on us. We had gone to the market expecting to see hundreds of those gentle, curvaceous beasts. But in that huge square we had found only one, on three legs, captive, living its last hour, and as it fought for its life we had driven away.[24]

The lure of such desolation is too strong for Canetti to resist, and the two companions return once more to the market. Here they find another tortured beast, growling at its captors, pitiably attempting to resist their efforts to still it:

> Of the two or three other people busying themselves at the animal's head one stood out particularly: a powerful stocky man with a dark cruel face . . . With brisk movements of his arm he was drawing a rope through a hole he had bored in the animal's septum. Nose and rope were red with blood. The camel flinched and shrieked, now and then uttering a great roar; finally, it leaped to its feet again, having by now knelt down, and tried to tug itself free, while the man pulled the rope tighter and tighter.[25]

There is no doubt at all where the reader's sympathies are meant to fall. The camel is the victim of inhuman treatment, unable to free itself from the despotic hold of the Moroccan man. The man is cruel – his cruelty such an innate trait that it is apparent in his very features. *He* is bestial, while the camel has human dimensions in that it is struggling for its freedom, trying in vain to escape the pain being inflicted upon it. This is the traditional view of the Oriental as despot, as cruel being and violent captor. He is not perturbed by blood or by the suffering of animals. Here is Richard Burton expressing this same sentiment a century earlier:

> We often see needless thrusts and blows, which disgust the least humane; and the use of the whip, especially when the driver appears in the semi-bestial negro shape, is universally excessive.[26]

Canetti returns to this theme of suffering animals in another chapter of his travelogue. This time the victim is a donkey, being harassed by one man while a crowd of others look on: 'They were all standing. The dark shadows on faces and figures, edged by the harsh light thrown on them by the lamps, gave them a cruel, sinister look.'[27] And the donkey?

> Of all the city's miserable donkeys, this was the most pitiful. His bones stuck out, he was completely starved, his coat was worn off, and he was clearly no longer capable of bearing the least little burden. One wondered how his legs still held him up . . . The music played on and on and the men, who now never stopped laughing, had the look of man-eating or donkey-eating savages.[28]

But despite the pathos of this description, the donkey had not been broken completely by the 'donkey-eating savages' at whose mercy it was. Canetti (who seems to have spent most of his time in Morocco tracking after tortured animals) returns in daylight to witness what he thinks a curious transformation. Before him stands the same creature, but visibly changed:

> He had not budged, but it was no longer the same donkey. Because between his back legs, slanting forwards and down, there hung all of a sudden a prodigious member. It was stouter than the stick the man had been threatening him with the night before.[29]

Running short of destitute animals, Canetti now turns his attention to the natives. The blind beggars fascinate him; he stands transfixed before their huddled forms. The beggar children that frequent the street where he lunches attract him. They become a part of his daily ritual, and he feels their absence acutely when they do not appear:

> I liked their lively gestures, the tiny fingers they pointed into their mouths when with pitiful expressions they whined 'Manger! manger!', the unspeakably sad faces they pulled as if they were on the verge of collapse from weakness and starvation.[30]

There is a theatricality about this poverty as Canetti sees it that is endearing. The gesture becomes more impressive than the meaning behind it. The spectacle of begging itself, usually so guilt-inducing, is made into an entertaining and light-hearted skit instead.

Canetti soon comes face to face with a different kind of beggar, who produces in him a totally different response. This is the 'marabout' to whom a chapter is devoted. Canetti discovers him in the bazaar, notices that he is blind and in rags, with a paralysed hand and a mouth that never stops chewing. The chewing is what captivates Canetti, and he approaches and offers the man a coin. Now the theatricality of poverty – of Eastern poverty – looms very large indeed; the marabout takes the proffered coin and puts it into his mouth:

> Hardly was it inside before he began chewing again. He pushed the coin this way and that in his mouth and it seemed to me I could follow its movements . . . I tried to dissolve my disgust at this proceeding in its outlandishness. What could be filthier than money? But this old man was not I; what caused me disgust gave him enjoyment, and had I not seen people kissing coins? The copious saliva undoubtedly had a role to play here, and he was clearly distinguished from other beggars by his ample generation of saliva.[31]

There is a curious mixture of themes here. It is a spectacle of very little appeal, but of great dramatic value. This is the East where revolting things take place, revolting things with a hidden significance not immediately comprehensible to the astonished outsider. Canetti soon assumes that the marabout is blessing the coin, extending in so doing some of his mystical powers towards the benefactor. Holiness and the physically repulsive are merged in a way that is supposedly truly Oriental. Doughty had described the Arab as a man sitting in excrement, whose brows touched heaven. Canetti merely harps on similar imagery. His holy man, like Lane's, is an aberration; he induces disgust and awe in equal proportions. He is one more oddity in this field of oddities, this Orient so lush in drama. He has no real counterpart in the Occident, for he is the opposite of all that is rational, possible, predictable, and, one may add, hygienic! Canetti tempers the disgust he feels by rationalising that this man was not he, was ruled by passions and governed by feelings unknown to him. Thus the iron distinction falls once again: the East and its abnormalities are distinct and removed from the sane and rational West.

This East, as traditional European accounts of it have stated, is hushed into a disturbing silence. This silence accompanies even the most mundane acts. Canetti sees it as part of a market scene. Here is his description of the poultry stall:

> When women approached they held the hens out to them to feel. The woman took the bird in her hand without the Berber's releasing it, without its altering its position. She pressed it and pinched it, her fingers going straight to the places where it ought to be meaty. No one said a word during this examination, neither the Berber nor the woman; the bird too remained silent.[32]

Canetti must have encountered a most taciturn fowl if one is to believe such a description of chicken-purchasing. But the silence he professes to witness is only a manifestation of a certain construct fundamental to Europe's Orient: it is the correlate of the closedness of the society, the secretiveness of all its significant aspects. Canetti on perusing the goods laid out for inspection at the market can only think of all the details that are enclosed, invisible, shut away from his curious gaze:

> In a society that conceals so much, that keeps the interior of its houses, the figures and faces of its women, and even its places of

worship hidden from foreigners, this greater openness with regard to what is manufactured and sold is doubly seductive.[33]

This enclosed society, according to Canetti, sublimates what it hides, transferring the qualities of all that is hidden onto exposed objects. Thus, in his description of bread being sold by veiled women, we find him transferring the sexuality of the women which he senses but cannot perceive onto the rounded loaves:

> There was something naked and alluring about those loaves; the busy hands of women who were otherwise shrouded except for their eyes communicated it to them. 'Here, this I can give you of myself; take it in your hand, it comes from mine.'[34]

The journey through Marrakesh is charged with this sense of transferred sexuality. Walking through the alleys of the Jewish Quarter, he peers into the private courtyards in order to see the inside of this world that shuts him out. His curiosity soon bears fruit: one occupant asks him inside, and he enters a house where a newly-wed woman is sitting in the courtyard. Canetti looks at her with fascination, presuming that she is as fascinated about him as he is about her: 'My curiosity about her was as great as hers about me. It had been her eyes that had drawn me into the house, and now she was staring at me in a steadfast silence as I chattered away, though not to her.'[35] This entrance into the private quarters of a Moroccan home opens up further entries; Canetti's host, having befriended him, takes him on to meet the rest of his family. Canetti meets a relative for whom he feels attraction (presuming once again that it is a reciprocated attraction):

> She was a well-developed young woman and she was looking at me in a wondering and far from servile way. She put me in mind at first glance of the kind of oriental women Delacroix painted. She had the same straight, slightly overlong nose. I was standing very close to her in the tiny courtyard and our glances met in response to a natural pull. I was so affected that I dropped my eyes, but then I saw her strong ankles, which were as attractive as her face.[36]

A great part of the woman's appeal is her ability to fit in with the

ideas of 'Oriental' beauty that Canetti is already familiar with
from the paintings of Delacroix. Thus the imagination's seraglio
opens briefly to admit the traveller who finds himself
overwhelmed by its pull, having encountered within it the kind of
apparition he indeed expected. But the attraction remains
unconsummated – no words are exchanged, no possibility of
reunion contemplated. The impossibility of possession is what
makes the woman so desirable and the whole encounter so
charged with eroticism.

On another occasion, Canetti sees an unveiled woman looking
down at him from a window. She speaks to him in a voice 'with so
caressing a quality in it that she might have been holding my head
in her arms'.[37] He remains transfixed beneath her window, unable
to tear himself away from such a vision. Hours pass, and he
remains there. 'How can I describe the effect that an unveiled
female face, looking down from the height of a window, has on one
in this city, in these narrow streets?'[38] But the effect is obvious
from the expectation of sexuality where sexuality is covered,
sheltered, forbidden. The eye creates it, magnifies its appeal,
makes the encountered woman 'more important than anything
else that this city might have to offer'.[39] The superb irony that
Canetti soon discovers is that this unveiled woman is insane.

Morocco for Canetti provides endless images of poverty,
disease, sorcery, superstition and sexuality. It is almost as if his
eye were searching out the instances of differentness that he could
present an audience with, in order to evoke shock, disgust,
laughter or pity. Canetti describes a string of beggars: a black man
selling coal, a one-eyed man selling vegetables, a decrepit man
selling stones. 'Before long, though, I was prepared for anything,
and it caused me no particular surprise to see an aged and infirm
man squatting on the ground and offering for sale a single,
shrivelled lemon.'[40] The book ends with the most extraordinary
'beggar' of all. Canetti describes a brown bundle in the middle of a
square which emits one single sound, 'a deep, long-drawn-out,
buzzing "e–e–e–e–e".'[41] He is both horrified and amazed at this,
returning every evening to look at it, and every evening finding it
still there:

The brown, soiled cloth was pulled right down over the head
like a hood, concealing everything. The creature – as it must
have been – squatted on the ground, its back arched under the

material. There was not much of a creature there, it seemed
slight and feeble, that was all one could conjecture . . . I never
saw it come, I never saw it go; I do not know whether it was
brought and put down there or whether it walked there by
itself.[42]

This 'creature' became the most powerful symbol of Canetti's
journey, the sound it uttered was so diligent and persistent that it
outlived all others.[43] And on this particular note, the book ends,
having exhausted Marrakesh's supply of miserable animals,
destitute natives, and decrepit 'creatures'.

From Canetti's encounter with the East, we turn to V. S.
Naipaul's. In *An Area of Darkness* (1964), *India: A Wounded
Civilization* (1977), and *Among the Believers* (1981), Naipaul
journeys through India first, then through Egypt, Iran, Pakistan,
Malaysia and Indonesia, weaving a narrative that seeks to
illuminate the 'area of darkness' that Naipaul's East represents.
Naipaul approaches India with trepidation, for it contains all that
he has tried to outgrow, rise above, reject. It is the country from
which his grandfather emigrated to set up a new life as an
indentured labourer in Trinidad. It is the country that lived on in
ritual, in food, in objects and family traditions. But it was a
country that had become peculiarly transformed in the oceanic
crossing: the real Uttar Pradesh had calcified into mere artefact
and the remnants of ritual – Trinidad had taken over completely.
Thus, on visiting India for the first time, Naipaul feels no sense of
belonging. He comes away with an acute sense of his separateness.
Like the British writers of the Raj, Naipaul sees himself as
someone who, although 'involved' with India, belongs to a
different world. It is not sheer coincidence that Naipaul finds
Kipling's writings about India perceptive and unmatched for
their accuracy; they happen to describe, as accurately as he would
wish, the alienated India he finds himself in:

It was all there in Kipling, barring the epilogue of the Indian
inheritance. A journey to India was not really necessary. No
writer was more honest or accurate; no writer was more
revealing of himself and his society.[44]

Naipaul's East is one he had extracted from his education, like any
Westerner. He had referred to a 'colonial, Trinidad-American,

English-speaking prejudice'[45] which kept him from being able to fully accept some aspects of India's legacy. He saw mainly what he expected to see, what he had been taught he would see. The East was a construct that had been whole in his mind before he ever embarked on the journey to it, and one that would hardly alter at all despite the journey taken. Arriving in Alexandria from Greece, he instantly perceives a shift from the Hellenic into the Oriental so clearly divided in his education; 'it was clear that here, not in Greece, the East began: in this chaos of uneconomical movement, the self-stimulated din, the sudden feeling of insecurity, the conviction that all men are not brothers and that luggage was in danger'.[46] Any British district commissioner would have found such sentiments expressive of his own feelings: the East was chaotic, noisy, frightening, despotic and full of thieves – on the whole, a loathsome place that had to be kept under control. This is Naipaul describing his entry into Egypt:

> Feature by feature, the East one had read about. On the train to Cairo the man across the aisle hawked twice, with an expert tongue rolled the phlegm into a ball, plucked the ball out of his mouth with thumb and forefinger, considered it, and then rubbed it away between his palms.[47]

This was the archetypal native of the Western imagination engrossed in his revolting habits. No contemporary European writer would have dared such a description (which would have been in complete keeping a few decades ago), but Naipaul feels within his rights to offer whatever description suits his prejudice – for after all, he is 'involved' with this East, having emerged from it and having 'made good'. Like working-class writers who achieve success with a middle-class readership since they offer an insider's description of the drunkenness or laziness of the class they now affect to despise, Naipaul uses his heritage to abuse its backwardness and prove his own sophistication. He is no longer of it: he has become rational, hygienic, educated, *civilised*. But the heritage still serves, since it can entertain, disgust and sadden his readers. He, however, is wise to it all, as sarcastic as befits one trained in the colonialist's tongue.

Naipaul believes that India's problems are neither economical nor political but psychological.[48] Indians are unable to see themselves, for they are immersed in a static culture, overwhelmed by despair. Naipaul believes that there is a philosophy of despair that is particularly Indian. This is merely a reiteration of the traditional Western concept of Eastern despair, Eastern fatalism, Eastern unworldliness. This philosophy led to failure, to 'passivity, detachment, acceptance'.[49] Indians could not redress their country's miseries because they could not locate them. They were too far gone in blindness, in self-deception. Naipaul adopts the clinical tone of the psychoanalyst – professional, perceptive, unerring and self-conscious of its own superior state of mind.

The Indian who was able to see India clearly was Mahatma Gandhi,[50] who, like Naipaul, had acquired civilisation abroad. Like the author, Gandhi had been formed by his experiences in an Indian emigré community away from the sub-continent (South Africa in Gandhi's case). He arrived in India at the age of forty-seven already developed: he had been a colonial, had been schooled in a Christian ethic, was, in short, of the West as well.[51] Being so schooled, he possessed the mental tools necessary for charting a course of pragmatic action for India. Yet even with such tools as Gandhi possessed he was defeated by India, transformed into a figure of reverence, incorporated into the slothful despair of a failed continent. Even Gandhi, as Naipaul sees it, was made useless despite his revolutionary Western vision, and turned Eastern.

Naipaul stresses that what Gandhi had criticised about India forty years ago still holds. For part of India's tragedy, as he sees it, is its stagnation. It is caught in a web of static misery. The Indians do not sense their plight, and this shortcoming on their part becomes a twisted sort of blessing.

It is well that Indians are unable to look at their country directly, for the distress they would see would drive them mad. And it is well that they have no sense of history, for how then would they be able to squat amid their ruins, and which Indian would be able to read the history of his country for the last thousand years without anger and pain?[52]

These natives who 'squat' (for natives invariably squat) in the midst of their historic tragedy are happily oblivious to its full significance. Like the child-like primitives that Western anthropology describes, Naipaul's Indians remain ignorant, innocent, passive and fatalistic. They are part of fatalistic Asia, part of the Eastern failure.

Naipaul journeys to a medieval town to watch a Shiite ceremony. He perceives the scene around him as static, as archaic ('it might have been of medieval Europe'):

> It was a town, damp or dusty, of smells: of bodies and picturesque costumes discoloured and acrid with grime, of black, open drains, of exposed fried food and exposed filth; a town of prolific pariah dogs of disregarded beauty below shop platforms, of starved puppies shivering in the damp caked blackness below butchers' stalls hung with bleeding flesh; a town of narrow lanes and dark shops and choked courtyards, of full, ankle-lengthed skirts and the innumerable brittle, scarred legs of boys.[53]

The town, like the whole of the East, is a jumble of contradictory and disturbing images; filth, food, beauty, blood – it is a spectacle as far removed from the sanitised West that the speaker affiliates himself with as any nightmare. Naipaul recounts, in the dry, unperturbed tone that Lane had used to describe Egypt, the bloody ceremony and the physical repulsiveness of its participants:

> As disquieting as the blood were the faces of some of the enthusiasts. One had no nose, just two punctures in a triangle of pink mottled flesh; one had grotesquely raw bulging eyes; there was one with no neck, the flesh distended straight from cheek to chest.[54]

This was the diseased spectre of the East rising before the onlooker, its leprous features blotting out all else. Naipaul chooses singular images to delineate this alien landscape, to transform it into a *tableau vivant* that would horrify and trouble a bourgeois audience, as in the following description of poverty in an Indian village among the ruins:

> A child was squatting in the mud of the street; the hairless, pink-skinned dog waited for the excrement. The child big-bellied, rose; the dog ate. Outside the temple there were two

wooden juggernauts decorated with erotic carvings: couples engaged in copulation and fellatio: passionless, stylized.[55]

The Indians could not see the startling poverty they were surrounded by, for they had become immune to its connotations. But it was different for Naipaul: 'I had learned to see; I could not deny what I saw. They remained in that other world.'[56]

Naipaul's 'area of darkness' has inhabitants who, with their quaint clothes and amusing phraseology, offer the necessary comic relief in a fashion made famous by Kipling. Naipaul cannot resist the stereotype of the 'funny foreigner', although his descriptions often verge on the pathetic rather than being merely droll. Naipaul's hostess, Mrs Mahindra, for example, marvels at his suitcase's content, fingering with great reverence all its imported goods. '"I am craze for foreign", Mrs Mahindra said. "Just craze for foreign." '[57] And the steward of a hotel where Naipaul stays offers the author an opportunity to make him into a figure of fun because of his peculiar use of English:

> 'Hot box coming next week,' Aziz said.
> 'Hot box?'
> 'Next week.' His voice was low; he was like a sweet-tempered nurse humouring a spoilt and irascible infant. He took a napkin off his shoulder and flicked away tiny flies. 'This is nothing. Get little hot, little flies dead. Big flies come chase little flies. Then mosquito come bite big flies and they go away.'[58]

Naipaul's 'Islamic journey' begins with his encounter with Sadeq, an Iranian interpreter whom he meets upon his arrival in Teheran:

> He came some minutes before eight. He was in his late twenties, small and carefully dressed, handsome, with a well-barbered head of hair. I didn't like him. I saw him as a man of simple origins, simply educated, but with a great pride, deferential but resentful, not liking himself for what he was doing. He was the kind of man who, without political doctrine, only with resentments, had made the Iranian revolution.[59]

This initial feeling sets the emotional tone for Naipaul's encounter with all the other individuals he will describe in the course of a long journey; although he is not always as hostile as he is in this first encounter, his sympathies are always limited – he is mostly pitying, deprecating, and always condescending. Naipaul reproduces conversations he has with Muslims during his journey in a manner that makes them come out sounding naive, absurd and intellectually moronish. Indeed, he perceives Islam itself as an expression of failure, of enraged failure. The religious fervour he sees in Pakistan only confirms his prejudice: 'failure led back again and again to the assertion of the faith'.[60] Islam was merely a refuge from distress,[61] it achieved nothing, but was parasitic and uncreative.[62]

The confusion Naipaul remarks in some of the young men he 'interviews' strikes responsive chords in him and takes him back to his own confused youth in colonial Trinidad. In conversation with one Malaysian who is describing to the author his complicated family background and the emotional turbulence which that engenders, Naipaul retorts: ' "In what way were you confused? My background is more complicated than yours, but I am not confused. And there are many people like me. Many people in the world today have complicated backgrounds." '[63] Naipaul had overcome confusion and intellectual turmoil once and for all: the Western education he had received had ensured that he was now rational, secure, capable of transcending the weighty burdens of an Eastern past. Whereas the Muslims he meets, with their frantic rejection of the West and all its secular gifts (a rejection that Naipaul neither understands nor forgives), are moved by passion and driven by rage:

> Their rage – the rage of a pastoral people with limited skills, limited money, and a limited grasp of the world – is comprehensive. Now they have a weapon: Islam. It is their way of getting even with the world. It serves their grief, their feeling of inadequacy, their social rage and racial hate.[64]

Naipaul sees only negativity in Islam. It is a religion of fanaticism that leads to a sensation of utter futility. It is an archaic form of devotion in a rapidly progressing world. It is symptomatic of a renunciation of civilisation that can only marginalise those who are renouncing it by placing them in an intellectual vacuum from which there is no escape. For Naipaul, any attempt to seek an

Islamic alternative to the Western pattern of social behaviour is an aberration, a contemptible failing in sophistication and skill.

Of the four Muslim countries he visits (Iran, Pakistan, Malaysia, Indonesia), only one country (Indonesia) elicits a sympathetic response from him. This is because that country appears in his eyes to be only superficially Muslim, because it has a population of non-Muslim peoples, and a cultural tradition that contains strong non-Islamic elements. And the only articulate and convincing person that Naipaul describes among all the 'believers' he meets, as opposed to the diminished dolts whose quaint and ridiculous ideas he takes so much pleasure in reproducing, the only man who comes near to achieving equal standing with Naipaul is the Indonesian poet, Sitor Situmorang. This man was not a Muslim, but belonged to an animist tribe in Sumatra, had received a sound Dutch education, and was married to a Dutch woman. Unlike the many Muslims Naipaul encounters who had all been intellectually and emotionally lost, Situmorang was placid and sane. He had achieved that calm by retrieving the heritage of his ancestors with the help of a European anthropologist (the antidote – as Naipaul sees it – to confusedness and frenzy).[65]

Despite his feelings of discomfort, anger, pity and frustration throughout the journey, Naipaul does allow himself to be seduced, if only once, by an Eastern location. Visiting a mountainous region in Pakistan, he comes across nomadic tribes of Afghans driving their sheep. Naipaul is enchanted by the scene: he is instantly transported to a familiar (familiar from literature) East which he finds pleasantly seductive. The spell that it casts over him 'brought to mind Tolstoy's and Lermontov's tales of the Caucasus'.[66] The scene fulfils Naipaul's expectations, taking him back to childhood's images, to the East of text-books, picturesque, unthreatening:

> The Afghan encampment had taken me back to the earliest geography lessons of my childhood, to the drawings in my *Homes Far Away* text-book: men creating homes, warmth, shelter in extreme conditions: the bow-and-arrow Africans in their stockades, protected against the night-time dangers of the forest; the Kirghiz in their tents in the limitless steppes; the Eskimoes in their igloos in the land of ice.[67]

The women perceived in this encampment have all the beauty necessary to the 'romantic' nature of such a vision; they make 'a peasant or nomadic longing' stir within Naipaul.[68] But the vision, although aesthetically pleasing, is nevertheless a static one possessing mere momentary charm. Naipaul senses the fragility of the attraction he feels:

> I would move on, do other things; they would continue as I saw them. And those girls, pretty as they were, with their lovely skins, were really far away, shut off in their own tribal fantasies, beauties now, well fed, conscious of their rising price, but soon to be wives and workers.[69]

The image serves its evocative purposes and then disintegrates: the speaker is left with a sense of his own removedness and isolation from what he sees. He moves on, having peered briefly into the static human past.

And it is with this sense of isolation that Naipaul's book ends; his journey's progress had been continually impeded by fear – fear not only of the chaos that he saw surrounding him, but also of how that very chaos could return him to the pain of his own colonial past. Thus, his rejection of the world he has passed through is a very forceful one indeed, since he must at all costs avoid being sucked back into it having once escaped it. He must remain separate from it, detached from its tragic turbulence and its traditions; he can 'survive' the journey East only by negating all that he sees, reducing it to a distant and deplorable 'area of darkness'. This fear, which produces prejudices and hostile beliefs, limits his perception and alienates him from the landscape before him. He returns from the journey still unchanged, and perhaps the worse for such lack of transformation.

Conclusory Remarks:
The Innocents Abroad?

Travelers renting Mongolian yurts discovered that the tent-like structures were made of plastic, not animal skin. And some visitors complained that the locals had become too Westernized. 'They're about as Mongol as I am,' said one vacationer from Miami.

'Vacations of a Lifetime'
Newsweek (7 June 1982)

In 1762, Oliver Goldsmith wrote a brilliant parody of the epistolary genre and Orientalism too which he entitled *Citizen of the World*. He adopted the trope made famous a few decades earlier by Montesquieu, and conceived of an Easterner writing home his observations of Europe. Goldsmith's Citizen is a studious, cultured, polite and reserved man, in fact, as unlike the traditional stereotype of the 'Oriental' as can be imagined. This, he soon discovers, is a shortcoming on his part, for he repeatedly disappoints his European hosts who find him wanting in barbarity. Their demand is for an *Oriental* Oriental, for a Picturesque addition to their eighteenth-century drawing-rooms. They have very little sympathy for this person so like themselves, so contrary to their preconceptions, whose 'very visage has nothing of the true exotic barbarity'.[1] Thus the 'Citizen of the World' leaves the Salons of Europe cold; he writes home of their grudgeful and fast-waning hospitality: '. . . nor was I invited to repeat my visit, because it was found that I aimed at appearing rather a reasonable creature than an outlandish idiot.'[2]

The European seemed constantly to transfer from one set of contradictory expectations to another. Either the Orient was not 'Oriental' enough, or it was *too* 'Oriental'. Either the journey to it was disappointing because it was already traversed by Occidental influence, or it was deplorable since it was so removed from all things Occidental so as to seem mere negation and banishment. The same traveller could simultaneously entertain such extremes of emotions. Napoleon wanted Egypt to be even more exotic than he found it, while condemning that very exoticism that left it a country ungraced by civilisation of a Western type, where he found neither *'fourchettes ni contesses'*.

The historical animosity between Christian Occident and Muslim Orient gradually changed, as the Ottoman threat grew continually less threatening, into a fascinated distrust instead. And it was precisely with this shift in attitude brought about by political circumstances that the literary fabrication of the Orient became invaluable to the Western imagination. The more fully the Orient fell under the sway of the European powers, the deeper it came to be sublimated in the imagination, in literature, painting, music, and fashion. The *Arabian Nights* appeared in Europe at a time that coincided with Turkish defeat. 'Turkish Rondos' were incorporated into European music when the Ottomans had ceased being a real threat to Europe's stability. And after Napoleon's conquest of Egypt, turbans were all the rage in the West. A shift in attitude had become strikingly visible by the nineteenth century; an ignorant awe had become a familiar contempt.

This new attitude became powerfully operative in the process of social and cultural definition. Stereotypes were forged and meanings instituted that were reciprocally confirming. The 'ideology' of Orientalism was inextricably tied to Western hegemony, yet it was not always expressed or articulated in the common forms of manipulation or indoctrination. It was a more subtle system of beliefs which was part of an intentionally selective tradition. It was a powerful system, nonetheless, since it was tied to many practical and directly experienced processes – religion, place, family, institution, and language. The West had to reshape the Orient in order to comprehend it; there was a sustained effort to devise in order to rule.

Orientalist studies were officially inaugurated by Sir William Jones, a servant of the East India Company, in order to deepen Europe's acquaintance with the peoples over whom it would ultimately come to have control. Europe could now afford to study the East calmly and carefully, and as England was the chief world power, it naturally took the lead in this.

The efforts of individual travellers to 'study' what they saw and describe it to their countrymen was an undertaking that met with imperial approbation. For the travelogues – despite their diversity – ultimately served to bring the Empire home. However, the reality was often confused with the fabrication of an Orient so intrinsic a part of each traveller's imagination. The East became codified and static in ways that were final; no deeper perception was permissible, nor indeed possible given the weighty heritage of prejudice. Thus Curzon could write, as late as 1895, that Morier's *Hajji Baba* was an honest description of the 'unchanging characteristics of a singularly unchanging people'.[3]

Even those rare travellers who quarrelled with the set metaphors of Orientalism were unable to avoid some of its meanings. Albert Smith, as we have seen, mocked the pompousness of Eastern travelogues but ultimately restated many of their prejudices. Mark Twain, who made an all out effort to satirise the genre of the Eastern travelogue, managed only to confirm every prejudice in the book. And although he wanted to deromanticise the Orient completely, he did so perniciously, with no sympathy, and with inhuman humour. He peoples this particular Orient with funny foreigners who are dirty, lazy, ugly, stupid and boring. His tour, as narrated in *The Innocents Abroad* (1869), deflates the East in order to inflate the narrator's status as superior being in it.

It is unfortunate that the bulk of European travel narrative about the East was so strongly coloured by bias and supposition. The narrative did no doubt lead to an expansion in knowledge of the world, but it was a tainted knowledge that served the colonial vision. Some of that taint is with us still despite the passing of the colonial era in its more obvious forms. It is mandatory that we ultimately arrive at a less prejudiced sort of narrative in our descriptions of other peoples, other races, other religions. And one of the ways to do this is to continually question the testimony we have inherited, be it from the soldier, the scholar or the traveller. In questioning those notions that are supposed to prove how different we are as peoples, perhaps we may, with sympathy and effort, arrive at an understanding of how similar we are as humans in an increasingly complicated world.

Notes and References

INTRODUCTION

1. A reversal of this notion is possible for purposes of parody, as in the letters of Usbek and Rica in Montesquieu's *Lettres persanes* (Paris, 1721), where two travellers from the East write home their observations of Europe.
2. Nicholas Ziadeh, *Al-Jughrafiya wal Rahalat 'ind al'Arab* (Beirut, 1962) pp. 10–15.
3. Regis Blachère and Henri Darmann, *Extraits des Principaux Géographes Arabes du Moyen Age* (Paris, 1957) p. 11.
4. G. R. Tibbetts, *A Study of the Arabic Texts containing Material on South-East Asia* (London, 1979) p. 2.
5. Ibid., p. viii.
6. Blachère and Darmann, *Géographes Arabes*, p. 95.
7. *The Book of the Marvels of India*, translated by Peter Quennel (London, 1928) p. 164.
8. Ibid., p. 165.
9. Tibbetts, *South-East Asia*, p. 176.
10. Antonio Pigafetta, *Magellan's Voyage (A Narrative Account of the First Navigation)*, translated and edited by R. A. Skelton (London, 1969) p. 85.
11. W. Arens, *The Man-Eating Myth: Anthropology and Anthropophagy* (New York, 1979) p. 49.
12. Louise K. Barnett, *The Ignoble Savage: American Literary Racism, 1790–1890* (Connecticut, 1975) p. 5.
13. Theodore Roosevelt, *The Winning of the West* (New York, 1896) p. 90.
14. James Fennimore Cooper, *The Last of the Mohicans* (London, 1826; 3 vols) vol. I, pp. 134–5.
15. Arens, *The Man-Eating Myth*, p. 95.
16. *Women and Colonization: Anthropological Perspectives*, Mona Etienne and Eleanor Leacock (eds) (New York, 1980) p. 175.
17. For a full study of this subject, see Allen MacFarlane, *Witchcraft in Tudor and Stuart England* (London, 1970).
18. V. G. Kiernan, *The Lords of Human Kind: European Attitudes towards the Outside World in the Imperial Age* (London, 1969) p. 6.
19. On 22 July, 1920, after the battle of Maysalun.
20. Charles Batten, *Pleasurable Instruction: Form and Convention in Eighteenth-Century Travel Literature* (Berkeley, 1978) p. 15.
21. Hester Stanhope, Jane Digby, Isabel Burton, Lucie Duff Gordon, Emily Eden, Amelia Edwards, Mary Kingsley, Gertrude Bell and Freya Stark among them.

22. Brian V. Street, *The Savage in Literature* (London, 1975) p. 13.
23. Norman Daniel, *Islam, Europe and Empire* (Edinburgh, 1966) p. 53.
24. Alexander Kinglake, *Eothen* (London, 1898) p. 54.
25. Kinglake, *Eothen*, p. 126.
26. Ibid., p. 215.
27. Richard F. Burton, *Sindh and the Races that inhabit the Valley of the Indus* (London, 1851; 1973) p. 284.
28. Kiernan, *The Lords of Human Kind*, p. 316.
29. Edward W. Said, *Orientalism* (London, 1978). I am indebted to Professor Said's definition of Orientalism as a method of cataloguing the Orient that was inextricably linked to the imperialistic world-view.
30. François-René de Chateaubriand, *Itinéraire de Paris à Jérusalem* (Paris, 1811) p. 128.
31. As quoted in James Ballantine, *The Life of David Roberts, R.A., Compiled from his Journals and Other Sources* (Edinburgh, 1866) pp. 104–5.

1 LEWD SARACENS

1. See F. M. Donner, *The Early Islamic Conquests* (Princeton, 1981).
2. J. B. Friedman, *The Monstrous Races in Medieval Art and Thought* (Cambridge, Mass., 1981) p. 65.
3. Ibid., p. 67.
4. Norman Daniel, *Islam and the West: The Making of an Image* (Edinburgh, 1960) p. 270.
5. Ibid., p. 102.
6. Ibid., p. 270.
7. R. W. Southern, *Western Views of Islam in the Middle Ages* (Cambridge, Mass., 1980) p. 30.
8. Ibid., p. 31.
9. For a study of this narrative, see S. Tonguç, *The Saracens in the Middle English Charlemagne Romances* (London, 1958), and B. White, *Saracens and Crusaders: From Fact to Allegory* (London, 1969).
10. In the same manner that pioneer romances of America used the Indian as an occasion for white-man heroics; Barnett, *The Ignoble Savage*.
11. Dorothee Metlitzki, *The Matter of Araby in Medieval England* (New Haven, 1977) p. 160.
12. Ibid., p. 161.
13. *Bevis of Hampton*, MS 175 Caius College Library, Cambridge; L. A. Hibbard (ed.) *Sir Bevis of Hampton* (London, 1911).
14. Metlitzki, *The Matter of Araby*, p. 168.
15. M. D. Taseer, *India and the Near East in English Literature from the Earliest Times to 1924* (Cambridge PhD thesis 1936) p. 51.
16. *The Sowdone of Babylone*, edited anonymously (London, 1854).
17. Metlitzki, *The Matter of Araby*, p. 175.
18. *The King of Tars*, MS Bodley 3938. Published in J. Ritson (ed.) *Ancient English Metrical Romances* (London, 1802).
19. *Floris and Blauncheflur*, MS Gg. 4. 27 (II), Cambridge University Library, edited by A. B. Taylor (Oxford, 1927).

20. See P. Meyer, *Alexandre le Grand dans la Littérature du Moyen Age* (Paris, 1886); and G. Cary, *The Medieval Alexander* (Cambridge, 1956).
21. M. C. Seymour (ed.) *The Travels of Sir John Mandeville* (Oxford, 1968).
22. H. Cordier (ed.) *The Book of Ser Marco Polo etc.* (London, 1920).
23. H. Cordier (ed.) *Les Voyages en Asie au XIVe Siècle du Bienheureux Frère Odoric de Pordenone* (Paris, 1891).
24. See A. C. Wood, *History of the Levant Company* (London, 1964); and Sir William Foster, *England's Quest for Eastern Trade* (London, 1933).
25. Shakespeare, *Macbeth*, I, iii, 73–9.
26. Thomas Dallam, *Diary (1599–1600) of a Voyage to Constantinople* in J. T. Bent (ed.) *Early Voyages and Travels in the Levant* (London, 1893) pp. 74–5.
27. Alain Grosrichard, *Structure du serail* (Paris, 1979) p. 155.
28. Sir George Courthope, *Memoirs (1616–1685)*, ed. S. C. Lomas (London, 1907) p. 123.
29. Norman Daniel, *Islam, Europe and Empire* (Edinburgh, 1966) p. 18.
30. Charles Robson, *Newes from Aleppo* (London, 1628).
31. See E. Jones, *Othello's Countrymen: The African in English Renaissance Drama* (London, 1965), and S. C. Chew, 'Moslems on the London Stage', *The Crescent and the Rose: Islam and England during the Renaissance* (New York, 1937) pp. 469–538.
32. *Antony and Cleopatra*, ii, 121–2.
33. Ibid., II, iii, 39–42.
34. Ibid., IV, viii, 25–30.
35. I shall use the term 'Arabian Nights' since it is the more popular one in England, and since I am considering the *Arabian Nights* as an English text and more generally as a Western literary phenomenon. For a thorough examination of the history of the *Arabian Nights*, see Suheir al-Qalamawi, *Alf Laila wa Laila* (Cairo, 1959).
36. Mohamed Abdel-Halim, *Antoine Galland: Sa vie et son oeuvre* (Paris, 1964) p. 299.
37. *Cléomades*, or *Le Cheval de Fust*, a fantastic metrical Romance of the late thirteenth century, written by Adenet le Roi, in which a wooden horse carries its riders through a varied web of adventure.
38. A *Roman d'Amour* of the late Middle Ages, which contains details that can be traced to oriental sources, and to the *Alf Laila wa Laila* in particular. For further elaboration on Eastern influence, see Katherine T. Butler, *A History of French Literature* (London, 1923; 2 vols) vol. 1, pp. 31–3.
39. P. Rajna, *Le Fonti dell'Orlando Furioso* (Florence, 1900) pp. 436–55.
40. Maurice Bouisson, *Le Secret de Shéhérezade: les sources folkloriques des contes arabo-persans* (Paris, 1961) p. 227.
41. Antoine Galland, *Journal (1672–3)*, ed. by Charles Schéfer (Paris, 1881; 2 vols) vol. I, pp. 56–7.
42. For a list of these translations, see Abdel-Halim, *Antoine Galland* pp. 476–8.
43. Exactly how ambitious d'Herbelot's erudition was can be gauged from the full title of his *oeuvre*: *Bibliothèques Orientale ou Dictionnaire Universel, contenant généralement tout ce qui regarde la connoissance des Peuples de l'Orient. Leurs Histoires et Traditions (véritable ou fabuleuses). Leurs religions, sectes et politiques, Leurs gouvernement, loix, coutumes, Moeurs, Guerres, les Révolutions de leurs Empires; Leurs Sciences et leurs Arts, Leurs Théologie, Mythologie, Magie, Physique, Morale,*

Médécine, Mathématiques, Histoire naturelle, Chronologie, Geographie, Observations Astronomiques, Grammaire, et Réthorique. Les Vies et Actions Remarquables de leurs saints, docteurs, philosophes, Historiens, Poetes, Capitaines & de tous ceux qui se sont rendu illustres parmis eux, par leur Vertu, ou par leur Savoir; Des jugements critiques, et des extraits de tous leurs ouvrages. De leurs Traités, Traductions, Commentaires, Abrégés, Recueils de Fables, de Sentences, de Maximes, de Proverbes, de Contes, de bons Mots & de tous leurs Livres écrits en Arabe, en Persan, ou en Turc, sur toutes formes de Science, d'Arts, et de Proféssions, Preface by Antoine Galland (Paris, 1697; 2 vols).

44. Galland, *Journal*, vol. I, pp. 41–2.
45. Jean Chardin, *Voyage de Monsieur le Chevalier Chardin en Perse et Autres Lieux de l'Orient* (Amsterdam, 1686; 2 vols) vol. II, p. 279.
46. Galland, *Journal*, vol. II, p. 19.
47. Chardin, *Voyage*, vol. I, p. 44.
48. Ibid., vol. II, p. 17.
49. Ibid., vol. II, p. 280.
50. Richard Burton, *The Book of the Thousand Nights and a Night* (London, 1884–6; 17 vols) 'Terminal Essay', vol. VII, p. 238.
51. Chardin, *Voyage*, vol. II, p. 281.
52. Abdel-Halim, *Antoine Galland*, p. 108.
53. Ibid., p. 259.
54. Ibid., p. 193.
55. Antoine Galland, *Les Milles et une nuits* (first published Paris, 1704; 1979 edn, 2 vols) vol. I, p. 46.
56. Ibid., vol. I, p. 3.
57. Abdel-Halim, *Antoine Galland*, p. 135.
58. Henri Baudet, *Paradise on Earth: Some Thoughts on European Images of Non-European Man* (New Haven, 1965) pp. 38–41.
59. Voltaire's attitude remained tenaciously medieval, as illustrated in his play, *Le Fanatisme ou Mahomet* (Paris, 1743), where he describes the Prophet as an imposter and an abuser of power. Voltaire uses Islam in order to attack religion altogether, and the 'infâme' hegemony of the Church to which he was so passionately opposed.
60. Mary Wortley Montagu, *The Complete Letters* (Oxford, 1763; 2 vols) vol. I, p. 385.
61. Leila Ahmed, *Edward W. Lane* (London, 1978) p. 130.
62. Martha Pike Conant, *The Oriental Tale in England in the Eighteenth Century* (New York, 1908) p. 5.
63. Quoted in G. Audisio, *La Vie de Haroun al-Raschid* (Paris, 1930) p. 74.
64. Quoted in Burton Feldman and Robert Richardson, *The Rise of Modern Mythology* (Bloomington, 1972) p. 313.
65. Ernest Bernbaum, *Guide through the Romantic Movement* (New York, 1949) p. 11.
66. Bernard Blackstone, *The Lost Travellers: A Romantic Theme with Variations* (London, 1962) p. 26.
67. Chateaubriand, *Mémoires d'outretombe* (Paris, 1817; 1949; 2 vols) vol. 1, p. 218.
68. Alexander Pope, *Correspondence* (Oxford, 1956; 5 vols) vol. I, p. 368.
69. Ibid., p. 369.

70. Oliver Goldsmith, *Citizen of the World* (London, 1762) pp. 138–9.
71. First written in French in 1782. William Beckford, *Vathek: The English Translation by Samuel Henley (1783) and the Lausanne and Paris Editions* (1784). Reprinted in 3 vols (New York, 1972).
72. These books are mentioned as Beckford's sources in Henley's English version of *Vathek*.
73. J. W. Oliver, *The Life of William Beckford* (London, 1932) p. 101.
74. For a full study of this subject, see Conant, *The Oriental Tale*.
75. Oliver, *The Life of William Beckford*, p. 23.
76. L. Melville, *Life and Letters of William Beckford* (London, 1910) p. 82.
77. Oliver, *The Life of William Beckford*, p. 66.
78. For a fascinating description of this incident, see Bernard d'Astorg, *Les Noces Orientales* (Paris, 1980) pp. 149–52.
79. Oliver, *The Life of William Beckford*, p. 128.
80. Ibid., p. 285.
81. Ibid., p. 287.
82. Blackstone, *Lost Travellers*, p. 181.
83. Byron, *Letters and Journals*, edited by Leslie A. Marchand (London, 1980; 12 vols) vol. III, p. 101.
84. Victor Jacquemont, *Letters from India; describing a Journey during the years 1828–1831* (London, 1835; 2 vols) vol. I, p. 360.
85. Thomas Moore, *Poetical Works* (New York, 1854) p. 424.
86. Ibid., p. 210.
87. Mario Praz, *The Romantic Agony* (London, 1970) p. 11.
88. J. B. Beer, *Coleridge the Visionary* (London, 1959) p. 63.
89. Ibid., p. 221.
90. Geoffrey Yarlott, *Coleridge and the Abyssinian Maid* (London, 1967) p. 151.
91. Beer, *Coleridge the Visionary*, p. 108.
92. Coleridge, *Collected Letters*, edited by E. Griggs (Oxford, 1956; 2 vols) vol. I, p. 347.
93. Ibid.

2 THE TEXT AS PRETEXT

1. Richard Hole, *Remarks on the Arabian Nights' Entertainment* (London, 1797) p. 10.
2. Henry Torrens, *The Book of the 1001 Nights* (London, 1838; 2 vols) vol. 1, p. iii.
3. Edward W. Lane, *The Thousand and One Nights* (London, 1839–41; 3 vols) vol. 3, p. 686.
4. This is in the Bodleian Library: *The Draft of the Description of Egypt*, MS Eng. misc. d. 234.
5. Edward W. Lane, *Manners and Customs of the Modern Egyptians* (London, 1836; 1963) p. iii.
6. Ibid., p. 267.
7. Ibid.
8. James Aldridge, *Cairo* (London, 1969) p. 12.
9. Lane, *Modern Egyptians*, p. 379.

10. Ibid., p. 385.
11. Edward Said, *Orientalism*, p. 103.
12. *Modern Egyptians*, p. 257.
13. Ibid., pp. 295–6.
14. Ibid., p. 305.
15. Ibid., p. 304.
16. Ibid., p. 222.
17. Ibid., p. 228.
18. Joseph Pitts, *A Faithful Account of the Religion and the Manners of the Mahometans (1704)* (London, 1738) pp. 46–7.
19. *Modern Egyptians*, p. 221.
20. Ibid.
21. Ibid.
22. The Lexicon or the translations, that is.
23. Lord Cromer, *Modern Egypt* (London, 1908; 2 vols) vol. 2, p. 538.
24. Ibid., p. 567.
25. Lane, *The Thousand and One Nights*, vol. I, p. 26, n. 11.
26. Ibid., vol. 1, p. 213, n. 12.
27. Ibid., vol. 1, p. 231, n. 54.
28. Ibid., vol. 1, pp. 30–1.
29. Said, *Orientalism*, p. 162.
30. Ibid., p. 164.
31. Ibid., p. 164.
32. Letter to Robert Hay, 30 January 1832. Quoted in Ahmed, *Edward W. Lane*, p. 39.
33. Muhsin Jassim Ali, *Scheherazade in England* (Washington, 1981) pp. 93–4.
34. Kathryn Tidrick, *Heart-Beguiling Araby* (Cambridge, 1981) p. 66.
35. Richard Burton, *Selected Papers on Anthropology, Travel and Exploration* (London, 1924) p. 22.
36. Quoted in Fawn Brodie, *The Devil Drives* (London, 1967) p. 59.
37. Ibid., p. 60.
38. Richard Burton, *The Book of the Thousand Nights and a Night* (London, 1885–8; 17 vols) vol. I, p. 13.
39. Ibid., vol. I, pp. 71–2.
40. Ibid., vol. I, p. 287.
41. Lisa Jardine, *Still Harping on Daughters* (London, 1983) p. 169.
42. Burton, *Thousand Nights*, vol. I, p. 6.
43. Ibid., vol. x, p. 236.
44. Ibid., vol. I, p. 212.
45. Lane, *Modern Egyptians*, p. 296.
46. Ibid.
47. Lillian Faderman, *Surpassing the Love of Men* (New York, 1981) pp. 148–50.
48. Burton, *Thousand Nights*, vol. II, p. 234.
49. Ibid., vol. II, p. 234.
50. Ibid., vol. IV, pp. 234–5.
51. Richard Burton, *Personal Narrative of a Pilgrimage to Al-Madinah and Meccah* (London, 1855–6; 2 vols) vol. I, p. 9.
52. Burton, *Thousand Nights*, vol. I, p. xvii.
53. Thomas Assad, *Three Victorian Travellers* (London, 1964) p. 51.

54. The letters of Richard Burton to Richard Monckton Milnes are at the Wren Library, Trinity College, Cambridge.
55. In a letter of 26 April 1862.
56. A. Pope-Hennessey, *Monckton Milnes: The Flight of Youth* (London, 1963) pp. 67–9.
57. Edmond and Jules de Goncourt, *Journal: Mémoires de la vie Littéraire* (Paris, 1878; reprinted 1956; 4 vols) vol. i, p. 1053.
58. Ibid.
59. Ibid., pp. 1056–7.
60. Letter from Dahomey, dated 31 May 1863.
61. *Letters of A. C. Swinburne to Richard Monckton Milnes (and other correspondents)* (London, 1915) p. 124.
62. Ibid., p. 148.
63. Burton to Monckton Milnes, from Trieste, dated 15 June 1875.
64. Burton, *Thousand Nights*, vol. x, p. 234.
65. Ibid., p. 238.
66. *Thousand Nights*, vol. i, p. 191.
67. Burton, *Thousand Nights*, vol. iv, p. 227.
68. E. Hellerstein, L. Hume and K. M. Offen (eds) *Victorian Women* (London, 1981) p. 125.
69. Burton, *Thousand Nights*, vol. x, p. 235.
70. Ibid., p. 233.
71. *Thousand Nights*, vol. i, p. 125.
72. Ibid., p. 234.
73. Richard Burton, *Zanzibar* (London, 1872; 2 vols) vol. i, p. 184.
74. The words of Dr E. W. Cushing, as quoted in B. Ehrenreich and D. English, *Complaints and Disorders* (London, 1974) p. 35.
75. Talal Asad, *Anthropology and the Colonial Encounter* (London, 1973) pp. 13–15.
76. Richard Burton, *A Mission to Gelele, King of Dahomey* (London, 1864; 2 vols) vol. 2, p. 198.
77. George Stocking, *Race, Culture, and Evolution* (New York, 1968) p. 126.
78. John Haller, *Outcasts from Evolution* (Urbana, 1971) p. 51.
79. Burton, *Thousand Nights*, vol. viii, p. 86.
80. Burton, *The Perfumed Garden* (London, 1886) p. 6.
81. As quoted in Byron Farwell, *Burton* (New York, 1963) p. 399.
82. For a detailed analysis of these additions, see Yassin Salhani, *Richard Burton* (University of Saint Andrews PhD dissertation, 1978) pp. 245–9.

3   THE SALON'S SERAGLIO

1. Victor Hugo, *Odes et Ballades, et Les Orientales* (Paris, 1940) p. 403.
2. As quoted in Leila Ahmed, *Edward W. Lane*, p. 1.
3. The description is Bernard Shaw's, as quoted in Andrea Rose, *Pre-Raphaelite Portraits* (London, 1981) p. 9.
4. Oscar Wilde, *Collected Works* (London, 1980) p. 429.
5. For a study of different European portrayals of Salome, see Mario Praz, *The Romantic Agony*, Ch. 5.
6. Gustave Flaubert, *Oeuvres complètes* (Paris, 1951; 2 vols) vol. 2, p. 675.

7. Although the dance in European literature also has sexual undertones, the man in it is active participant, rather than voyeur (see *Madame Bovary, Anna Karenina, Tess of the D'Urbervilles*).
8. Norman Bryson, *Word and Image: French Painting of the Ancien Régime* (Cambridge, 1981) p. 92.
9. Jacques Bousquet, *Les themes du Rêve dans las Littérature Romantique* (Paris, 1964) p. 504.
10. Claude Pichois, *Baudelaire: Études et Temoignages* (Neuchatel, 1974) p. 20.
11. Tamara Bassim, *La femme dans l'oeuvre de Baudelaire* (Neuchatel, 1974) p. 20.
12. Bousquet, *Les themes*, p. 498.
13. Raymond Schwab, *La Renaissance Orientale* (Paris, 1950) p. 439.
14. Flaubert, *Correspondances* (Paris, 1902; 13 vols) vol. 2, p. 119.
15. Edmond et Jules de Goncourt, *Mémoires de la vie littéraire*, vol. 2, p. 156.
16. Jeanne Bem, *Désir et Savoir dans l'Oeuvre de Flaubert* (Neuchatel, 1979) p. 96.
17. Flaubert, *Oeuvres complètes*, vol. 1, p. 85.
18. Ibid., vol. 1, p. 81.
19. Ibid., vol. 2, p. 691.
20. Goncourt, *Mémoires*, vol. ii, pp. 21–2.
21. V. G. Kiernan, *The Lords of Human Kind*, p. 131.
22. As quoted in Bernard Delvaille, *Théophile Gautier* (Paris, 1968) p. 65.
23. Article in 'La Presse', 29 September 1851. Delvaille, p. 60.
24. The Orientalist painters became highly organised as their genre grew steadily more popular. Some of their Societies included the *Société des Peintres Orientalistes Français*, and the *Société des Peintres Algériens et Orientalistes* (for those wishing to work in North Africa).
25. Article in 'La Presse', 19 March 1845. Delvaille, *Théophile Gautier*, p. 93.
26. Article in 'Revue des Deux Mondes', 1 July 1848. Delvaille, *Théophile Gautier*, p. 18.
27. As quoted by Phillipe Jullian, *Les Orientalistes* (Paris, 1977) p. 72.
28. Ibid., p. 73.
29. Wilde, *Collected Works*, p. 425.
30. Jullian, *Les Orientalistes*, p. 40.
31. Mark Girouard, *The Return to Camelot: Chivalry and the English Gentleman* (London, 1981) p. 225.
32. Gerard de Nerval, *Oeuvres complètes* (Paris, 1961; 2 vols) vol. 2, p. 173.
33. Hugo, *Odes et Ballades*, p. 488.
34. Pierre Loti, *Aziyadé* (Paris, 1879) p. 56.
35. Nerval, *Oeuvres complètes*, vol. 2, p. 467.
36. William Makepeace Thackeray, *Notes of a Journey from Cornhill to Grand Cairo* (London, 1845) pp. 278–9.
37. Edward Lear, *Later Letters of Edward Lear*, edited by Lady Strachey (London, 1911) p. 91.
38. Thackeray, *Notes of a Journey*, p. 207.
39. Ibid., p. 209.

4 DOUGHTY TRAVELLERS

1. Byron Farwell, *Burton* (New York, 1963) p. 2.
2. William Hazlitt, *Table Talk* (London, 1821; 1960) p. 189.
3. Ibid., p. 188.
4. Lane, *Manners and Customs of the Modern Egyptians*, p. xxv.
5. Burton, *Personal Narrative of a Pilgrimage to Al-Madinah and Meccah*, vol. i, p. 114.
6. Peter Brent, *Far Arabia: Explorers of the Myth* (London, 1977) p. 178.
7. James Silk Buckingham, *Travels in Palestine* (London, 1821), p. xix.
8. Ahmed, *E. W. Lane*, p. 95.
9. Burton, *Pilgrimage*, vol. i, p. 114.
10. T. E. Lawrence, *Secret Dispatches from Arabia* (London, 1939) p. 27.
11. T. E. Lawrence, *Seven Pillars of Wisdom: A Triumph* (London, 1935; 1965) p. 29.
12. Ibid., p. 30.
13. Ibid., p. 176.
14. Ibid., p. 23.
15. Ibid., p. 28.
16. Burton, *Thousand Nights*, vol. i, p. 1.
17. Burton's letter to Monckton Milnes from Trieste, dated 15 June 1875. Mss. at Wren Library, Trinity College, Cambridge.
18. Quoted by Isabel Burton, *The Life of Capt. Sir Richard Burton* (London, 1893, 2 vols) vol. ii, p. 442.
19. The Blunts collected horses, and their cross-breeding produced the Crabbet Stud, considered a fine specimen of the pure Arab horse.
20. Wilfrid Scawen Blunt, *Secret History of the English Occupation of Egypt (Being a Personal Narrative of Events)* (London, 1895) p. 5.
21. Blunt, *Ideas about India* (London, 1885) p. 21.
22. Ibid., p. 47.
23. Ibid., p. 3–5.
24. Ibid., p. 161.
25. Ibid., p. 167.
26. Ibid., p. 168.
27. Blunt, *Secret History*, p. 92.
28. Lady Anne Blunt, *Bedouin Tribes of the Euphrates* (New York, 1879) p. 228. Wilfred Blunt wrote the preface, the postscript, and chapters 23 to 28 of this book.
29. Blunt, *The Future of Islam*, p. 44.
30. Blunt, *Secret History*, p. 156.
31. Blunt, *Atrocities of Justice under British Rule in Egypt* (London, 1906) p. 4.
32. Ibid., p. 49.
33. Ibid., p. 38.
34. Ibid., p. 41.
35. Ibid.
36. Ibid., pp. 55–6.
37. Ibid., p. 15.
38. Ibid., pp. 14–15.
39. Ibid., p. 22.
40. Albert Smith, *A Month at Constantinople* (London, 1850) p. viii.

41. Ibid., p. 99.
42. Ibid., p. 100.
43. Ibid., p. 108.
44. Ibid., p. 54.
45. Ibid., pp. 97–8.
46. Ibid., p. 51.
47. Ibid., p. 106.
48. Charles Doughty, *Travels in Arabia Deserta* (London, 1888; 1936; 2 vols) vol. I, p. 125.
49. Doughty, *Arabia Deserta*, Preface to the Third Edition.
50. *Arabia Deserta*, vol. I, p. 142.
51. Norman Daniel, *Islam, Europe and Empire* (Edinburgh, 1966) p. 246.
52. *Arabia Deserta*, vol. I, p. 551.
53. *Arabia Deserta*, vol. II, p. 66.
54. *Arabia Deserta*, vol. II, p. vii.
55. A. J. Arberry, *British Orientalists* (London, 1943) p. 22.
56. *Arabia Deserta*, vol. I, p. 443.
57. Ibid., p. 318.
58. *Arabia Deserta*, vol. II, p. 338.
59. *Arabia Deserta*, vol. I, p. 95.
60. T. E. Lawrence, Introduction to *Arabia Deserta*, vol. I, p. xxix.
61. Ibid., pp. xxix–xxx.
62. Ibid., p. xxxv.
63. *Arabia Deserta*, vol. II, p. 539.
64. Lawrence, *Seven Pillars*, p. 36.
65. Ibid., p. 41.
66. Ibid., p. 24.
67. *The Letters of T. E. Lawrence*, edited by David Garnett (London, 1938) p. 291.
68. Lawrence, *Seven Pillars*, p. 2.
69. *Seven Pillars*, Dedication.
70. *Seven Pillars*, p. 452.
71. As Desmond Stewart proves in his excellent biography of Lawrence, *T. E. Lawrence* (London, 1977) pp. 241–3.
72. One thing that all Lawrence's biographers affirm is his self-confessed and pronounced masochism.

5 AMONG THE BELIEVERS

1. Italo Calvino, *Invisible Cities* (New York, 1974) p. 69.
2. Ibid., p. 28.
3. Ibid., p. 86.
4. Wilfrid Thesiger, *Arabian Sands* (London, 1959; 1979) p. 11.
5. Ibid., p. 11.
6. Ibid., p. 12.
7. The term is Tidrick's, *Heart-Beguiling Araby*, p. 5.
8. Benjamin Disraeli, *Tancred* (London, 1847; 2 vols) vol. I, p. 150.
9. Thesiger, *Arabian Sands*, p. 15.

10. Ibid., p. 37.
11. Ibid., p. 35.
12. Ibid., p. 31.
13. Ibid., p. 39.
14. Ibid., p. 50.
15. Ibid., p. 53.
16. Ibid., p. 139.
17. Ibid., p. 135.
18. Ibid., p. 170.
19. Ibid., p. 206.
20. Ibid., p. 188.
21. Wilfrid Thesiger, *The Marsh Arabs* (London, 1964; 1980) pp. 105–7, Plates 36–7;
22. Victor Segalen, *Essai sur l'Exotisme* (Paris, 1978) p. 20.
23. Elias Canetti, *The Voices of Marrakesh* (London, 1982), p. 9.
24. Ibid., pp. 10–11.
25. Ibid., p. 15.
26. Richard Burton, *Sindh and the Races that Inhabit the Valley of the Indus* (London, 1851; 1973) p. 11.
27. Canetti, *Voices of Marrakesh*, p. 88.
28. Ibid., p. 88.
29. Ibid., pp. 89–90.
30. Ibid., p. 83.
31. Ibid., pp. 27–8.
32. Ibid., p. 44.
33. Ibid., p. 20.
34. Ibid., pp. 81–2.
35. Ibid., p. 56.
36. Ibid., pp. 67–8.
37. Ibid., p.34.
38. Ibid., p. 35.
39. Ibid., p. 36.
40. Ibid., pp. 41–2.
41. Ibid., p. 100.
42. Ibid., pp. 101–2.
43. Ibid., p. 103.
44. V. S. Naipaul, *An Area of Darkness* (London, 1964; 1981) p. 191.
45. Ibid., p. 190.
46. Ibid., p. 10.
47. Ibid., p. 12.
48. Ibid., p. 214.
49. Ibid., p. 188.
50. Gandhi's recent popularity in the Western media (the film *Gandhi*, for instance) has a great deal to do with his 'Christian' qualities; he is nonviolent, holy, forgiving, although at heart rebellious; he is the kind of 'native' that the European can tolerate, since his anger is controlled, contained. A more violent or anarchic Indian leader would certainly not have been viewed in as sympathetic a light, nor cast as the hero or the star of a commercial media venture. In the same manner, Martin Luther King has

been made into the token Black political figure by the American media, precisely because he advocated non-violence and forgiveness as Gandhi had done. His assimilation into the popular imagination has not, however, been as complete as that of Gandhi: he is too recent a political phenomenon, and a few shades darker too – two points which account for any continued uneasiness concerning his status in the Western pantheon of acceptable 'natives'.

51. Naipaul, *An Area of Darkness*, pp. 73–4.
52. Ibid., p. 112.
53. Ibid., p. 123.
54. Ibid., p. 127.
55. Ibid., p. 204.
56. Ibid., p. 213.
57. Ibid., p. 85.
58. Ibid., p. 105.
59. V. S. Naipaul, *Among the Believers: An Islamic Journey* (London, 1981) p. 8.
60. Ibid., p. 85.
61. Ibid., p. 228.
62. Ibid., pp. 158–9.
63. Naipaul, *Among the Believers*, p. 269.
64. Ibid., p. 214.
65. Ibid., p. 295.
66. Ibid., p. 177.
67. Ibid., p. 177.
68. Ibid., p. 177.
69. Ibid., p. 177.

CONCLUSORY REMARKS: THE INNOCENTS ABROAD?

1. Oliver Goldsmith, *Citizen of the World* (London, 1762) p. 135.
2. Ibid., p. 140.
3. G. N. Curzon, *Persia and the Persian Question* (London, 1892; 2 vols) vol. i, p. ix.

Bibliography

PRIMARY SOURCES

Beckford, William, *Vathek* (London, 1783).
Blunt, Wilfrid Scawen, *Ideas about India* (London, 1885).
——, *Atrocities of Justice Under British Rule in Egypt* (London, 1906).
——, *Secret History of the English Occupation of Egypt* (London, 1907).
Bruce, James, *Travels to Discover the Source of the Nile* (Edinburgh, 1790).
Buckingham, James Silk, *Travels in Palestine* (London, 1821).
Burckhardt, J. L., *Travels in Arabia* (London, 1829).
Burton, Richard Francis, *Scinde; or the Unhappy Valley* (London, 1851).
——, *Personal Narrative of a Pilgrimage to Al-Madinah and Meccah* (2 vols; London, 1855–6).
——, *First Footsteps in East Africa* (London, 1856).
——, *A Mission to Gelele, King of Dahomey* (London, 1864).
——, *Zanzibar; City, Island and Coast* (London, 1872).
——, *The Kasidah* (London, 1882).
——, *A Plain and Literal Translation of the Arabian Nights' Entertainments* (17 vols; London 1884–6).
Burton, Richard F. and F. F. Arbuthnot, *The Kama Sutra* (London, 1883).
Burton, Richard F. and Charles Tyrwhitt-Drake, *Unexplored Syria* (2 vols; London, 1872).
Byron, Lord George Gordon, *Letters and Journals* ed. L. A. Marchand (12 vols; London, 1980).
Byron, Robert, *The Road to Oxiana* (London, 1937).
Calvino, Italo, *Invisible Cities* (New York, 1974).
Canetti, Elias, *The Voices of Marrakesh* (London, 1982).
Carlyle, Thomas, *Heroes and Hero-Worship* (Boston, 1840).
Chardin, Jean, *Voyage de Monsieur le Chevalier Chardin en Perse et Autres Lieux de l'Orient* (2 vols; Amsterdam, 1686).
Chateaubriand, François-René de, *Itinéraire de Paris à Jérusalem* (Paris, 1811).
——, *Mémoires d'outretombe* (2 vols; Paris, 1817).
Coleridge, Samuel Taylor, *Collected Letters*, ed. E. L. Griggs (2 vols; Oxford, 1956).
——, *The Notebooks of Samuel Taylor Coleridge*, ed. Kathleen Coburn (2 vols; London, 1957–62).
——, *Collected Works*, ed. B. E. Rooke (2 vols; London, 1969).
Cooper, James Fennimore, *The Last of the Mohicans* (3 vols; London, 1826).
Courthope, George, *Memoirs (1616–1685)*, ed. S. C. Lomas (London, 1907).
Cromer, Lord Evelyn Baring, *Modern Egypt* (London, 1908).

Dallam, Thomas, *Diary (1599–1600) of a Voyage to Constantinople*, ed. J. T. Bent (London, 1893).

Delacroix, Eugène, *Oeuvres littéraires* (2 vols; Paris, 1923).

——, *Journal de Eugène Delacroix*, ed. André Joubin (3 vols; Paris, 1932).

D'Herbelot, Bartholomeo, *Bibliothèque orientale*, ed. Antoine Galland (2 vols; Paris, 1697).

Disraeli, Benjamin, *Tancred, or The New Crusade* (2 vols; London, 1847).

Doughty, Charles, *Travels in Arabia Deserta* (London, 1888).

Flaubert, Gustave, *Oeuvres complètes*, ed. R. Dumesnil (2 vols; Paris, 1954).

Fromentin, Eugène, *Un Été dans le Sahara* (Paris, 1857).

——, *Voyage en Egypte, 1869* (Paris, 1935).

Galland, Antoine, *Les Mille et une nuits* (12 vols; Paris, 1704–17).

——, *Journal (1672–1673)* ed. Charles Schéfer (2 vols; Paris, 1881).

Gautier, Théophile, *Voyages pittoresques en Algérie* (Paris, 1845).

——, *Constantinople* (Paris, 1856).

——, *Abécédaire du Salon de 1861, etc.* (Paris, 1861).

——, *Les Dieux et Demi-Dieux de la Peinture* (Paris, 1864).

Goldsmith, Oliver, *Citizen of the World* (London, 1762).

Haggard, Rider, *King Solomon's Mines* (London, 1885).

Hazlitt, William, *Table Talk* (London, 1821).

Hogarth, David, *The Penetration of Arabia* (Oxford, 1922).

Hole, Richard, *Remarks on the Arabian Nights' Entertainment* (London, 1979).

Hugo, Victor, *Odes et Ballades, et Les Orientales* (Paris, 1829).

Jacquemont, Victor, *Letters from India; describing a Journey during the years 1828–1831* (2 vols; London, 1835).

Jones, William, *Asiatic Miscellany* (2 vols; London, 1787).

Kinglake, Alexander, *Eothen* (London, 1844).

Lane, Edward William, *Manners and Customs of the Modern Egyptians* (London, 1836).

——, *The Thousand and One Nights* (3 vols; London, 1838–41).

——, *Selections from the Kur-an* (London, 1843).

——, *An Arabic–English Lexicon* (London, 1863–74).

Lawrence, T. E., *Seven Pillars of Wisdom: A Triumph* (London, 1935).

——, *The Letters of T. E. Lawrence* ed. David Garnett (New York, 1939).

——, *Secret Dispatches from Arabia* (London, 1939).

Lear, Edward, *Journals of a Landscape Painter in Greece and Albania etc.* (London, 1851).

——, *Letters of Edward Lear* ed. Lady Strachey (London, 1907).

——, *Later Letters of Edward Lear* ed. Lady Strachey (London, 1911).

Lewis, John Frederick, *Lewis's Illustrations of Constantinople, made . . . in the years 1835–6.* (London, 1837).

Loti, Pierre, *Aziyadé* (Paris, 1879).

——, *Roman d'un Spahi* (Paris, 1881).

——, *Fantôme d'Orient* (Paris, 1892).

——, *Le Mariage de Loti* (Paris, 1893).

——, *Vers Ispahan* (Paris, 1904).

Mandeville, Sir John, *Travels* ed. M. C. Seymour (Oxford, 1968).

Montagu, Mary Wortley, *The Complete Letters* (2 vols; Oxford, 1763).

Montesquieu, *Lettres persanes* (Paris, 1721).

Moore, Thomas, *Poetical Works* (New York, 1854).
Morier, James, *The Adventures of Hajji Baba of Ispahan* (London, 1914).
——, *The Adventures of Hajji Baba of Ispahan in England* (London. 1925).
Naipaul, V. S., *An Area of Darkness* (London, 1964).
——, *India: A Wounded Civilization* (London, 1977).
——, *Among the Believers: An Islamic Journey* (London, 1981).
Nefzawi, *The Perfumed Garden* ed. and trans. Richard Burton (London, 1886).
Nerval, Gerard de, *Oeuvres complètes* (2 vols; Paris, 1961).
Odoric, *Les Voyages en Asie au XIVe Siècle du Bienheureux Frère Odoric de Pordenone* ed. H. Cordier (Paris, 1891).
Payne, John, *The Book of the Thousand and One Nights* (9 vols; London, 1882–4).
Pigafetta, Antonio, *Magellan's Voyage* (*A Narrative Account of the First Navigation*) ed. and trans. R. A. Skelton (London, 1969).
Pitts, Joseph, *A Faithful Account of the Religion and Manners of the Mahometans* (London, 1731).
Polo, Marco, *The Book of Ser Marco Polo etc.* ed. H. Cordier (London, 1920).
Pope Alexander, *Correspondence* (5 vols; Oxford, 1956).
Prichard, James Cowles, *Researches into the Physical History of Mankind* (5 vols; London, 1826).
——, *The Natural History of Man* (London, 1843).
Purchas, *Purchas His Pilgrims* (London, 1625).
Roberts, David, *The Holy Land, Syria, Idumea, Arabia, Egypt and Nubia* (6 vols; London, 1842–9).
Robson, Charles, *Newes from Aleppo* (London, 1628).
Scott, Walter, *The Poetical Works of Sir Walter Scott* (London, 1894).
——, *The Waverley Novels* (12 vols).
Shakespeare, William, *Complete Works*, ed. J. D. Wilson (London, 1980).
Smith, Albert, *A Month at Constantinople* (London, 1850).
Stanley, H. M., *Through the Dark Continent* (London, 1878).
——, *How I found Livingstone* (London, 1872).
Sterne, Lawrence, *A Sentimental Journey* (London, 1768).
Swinburne, A. C., *The Complete Works* (London, 1925).
Thackeray, W. M., *Notes of a Journey from Cornhill to Grand Cairo* (London, 1848).
Thesiger, Wilfrid, *Arabian Sands* (London, 1959).
——, *The Marsh Arabs* (London, 1964).
Thomas, Bertram, *Arabia Felix* (London, 1932).
Torrens, Henry, *The Book of the Thousand and One Nights* (London, 1838).
Voltaire, *Le Fanatisme ou Mahomet* (Paris, 1763).
Wilde, Oscar, *Collected Works* (London, 1980).
Woolley, Leonard, *Dead Towns and Living Men* (London, 1920).

SECONDARY SOURCES

Abdel-Halim, Mohammad, *Antoine Galland, sa vie, et son oeuvre* (Paris, 1964).
Abdullah, Adel, *The Arabian Nights in English Literature to 1900* (Ph.D. Dissertation, Cambridge University, 1963).
Adams, Percy, *Traveller and Travel Liar* (*1600–1800*) (Los Angeles, 1962).
Ahmed, Leila, *Edward W. Lane* (London, 1978).

Aldington, Richard, *Lawrence of Arabia: A Biographical Enquiry* (London, 1969).
Aldridge, James, *Cairo* (London, 1969).
Allen, Walter, *Transatlantic Crossing* (London, 1971).
Annan, M. C., *The Arabian Nights in English Literature to 1900* (Ph.D Dissertation, Northwestern University, 1945).
Arberry, A. J., *British Orientalists* (London, 1943).
Archer, M., *India and British Portraiture, 1770–1825* (London, 1979).
Arens, W., *The Man-Eating Myth* (London, 1979).
Asad, Talal, *Anthropology and the Colonial Encounter* (London, 1973).
Assad, Thomas, *Three Victorian Travellers* (London, 1964).
Ballantine, James, *The Life of David Roberts, R.A. Compiled from his Journals and Other Sources* (Edinburgh, 1866).
Barnett, Louise K., *The Ignoble Savage: American Literary Racism, 1790–1890* (Connecticut, 1975).
Bassim, Tamara, *La femme dans l'oeuvre de Baudelaire* (Neuchatel, 1974).
Batten, Charles, *Pleasurable Instruction: Form and Convention in Eighteenth-Century Travel Literature* (Berkeley, 1978).
Baudet, Henri, *Paradise on Earth: Some Thoughts on European Images of Non-European Man* (New Haven, 1965).
Bearce, G. D., *British Attitudes towards India (1784–1858)* (Oxford, 1961).
Beer, J. P., *Coleridge the Visionary* (London, 1959).
Bem, Jeanne, *Désir et Savoir dans l'oeuvre de Flaubert* (Neuchatel, 1979).
Bénédite, Léonce, *Théodore Chassériau, sa vie et son oeuvre* (2 vols; Paris, 1932).
Bernbaum, Ernest, *Guide through the Romantic Movement* (New York, 1949).
Blachère, Régis and Henri Darmaun, *Extraits des Principaux Géographes Arabes du Moyen Age* (Paris, 1957).
Blackstone, Bernard, *Lost Travellers: A Romantic Theme with Variations* (London, 1962).
Bouisson, Maurice, *Le Secret de Shéhérazade: Les sources folkloriques des contes arabo-persans* (Paris, 1961).
Bousquet, Jacques, *Les themes du rêve dans la littérature romantique* (Paris, 1964).
Brent, Peter, *Far Arabia: Explorers of the Myth* (London, 1977).
Brodie, Fawn, *The Devil Drives* (London, 1967).
Broughton, Henry, *Lawrence of Arabia: The Facts without the Fiction* (Dorset, 1969).
Brownmiller, Susan, *Against our Will: Men, Women and Rape* (New York, 1975).
Bryson, Norman, *Word and Image: French Painting of the Ancien Régime* (Cambridge, 1981).
Burton, Isabel, *The Life of Capt. Sir Richard Burton* (London, 1983).
Butler, Katherine, *A History of French Literature* (2 vols; London, 1923).
Cannon, Garland H., *Oriental Jones: A Biography of Sir William Jones* (London, 1964).
Carré, Jean-Marie, *Voyageurs et écrivains français en Egypte* (Cairo, 1956).
Carrington, Dorothy, *The Traveller's Eye* (London, 1947).
Cary, G., *The Medieval Alexander* (Cambridge, 1956).
Charnay, J. P., *Les Contre-Orients* (Paris, 1980).
Chaumelin, Marius, *Decamps. Sa vie, son oeuvre, ses imitateurs* (Marseille, 1861).
Chew, Samuel, *The Crescent and the Rose* (New York, 1937).
Chinard, G., *L'Amerique et le rêve exotique* (Paris, 1913).

Christinger, Raymond, *Le Voyage dans l'imaginaire* (Paris, 1981).
Conant, Martha Pike, *The Oriental Tale in England in the Eighteenth Century* (New York, 1908).
Coulon, M., *Les vraies lettres de Rimbaud* (Paris, 1930).
Cruse, Amy, *The Englishman and His Books in the Nineteenth Century* (London, 1930).
——, *The Victorians and Their Books* (London, 1935).
Daniel, Norman, *Islam and the West: The Making of an Image* (Edinburgh, 1960).
D'Astorg, Bernard, *Les Noces Orientales* (Paris, 1980).
Davis, Angela, *Women, Race and Class* (London, 1982).
Dearden, Seton, *The Arabian Knight: A Study of Sir Richard Burton* (London, 1953).
Delamont, Sara and Lorna Dufflin (eds) *The Nineteenth-Century Woman* (London, 1978).
Delvaille, Bernard, *Théophile Gautier* (Paris, 1968).
De Meester, Marie, *Oriental Influences in the English Literature of the Nineteenth Century* (Heidelberg, 1915).
Donner, F. M. *The Early Islamic Conquests* (Princeton, 1981).
Dworkin, Andrea, *Pornography* (London, 1982).
Eliseef, N., *Themes et Motifs des Mille et une Nuits* (Beirut, 1949).
Etienne, Mona and Eleanor Leacock (eds) *Women and Colonization: Anthropological Perspectives* (New York, 1980).
Faderman, Lillian, *Surpassing the Love of Men* (New York, 1981).
Fairley, Barker, *Charles M. Doughty: A Critical Study* (London, 1927).
Farwell, Byron, *Burton* (New York, 1963).
Fedden, Robin, *English Travellers in the Near East* (London, 1958).
Feldman, Burton and Robert Richardson, *The Rise of Modern Mythology* (Bloomington, 1972).
Finch, Edith, *Wilfrid Scawen Blunt* (London, 1938).
Foster, William, *England's Quest for Eastern Trade* (London, 1933).
Friedman, J. B., *The Monstrous Races in Medieval Art and Thought* (Cambridge, Mass., 1981).
Froude, J. A., *Thomas Carlyle* (2 vols; London, 1884).
Gail, Marzieh, *Persia and the Victorians* (London, 1951).
Gaury, Gerald de, *Travelling Gent: The Life of Alexander Kinglake (1809–1891)* (London, 1972).
Gérin, Winifred, *Charlotte Brontë* (Oxford, 1967).
Girouard, Mark, *The Return to Camelot: Chivalry and the English Gentleman* (London, 1981).
Glen, Douglas, *In the Steps of Lawrence of Arabia* (London, 1941).
Goncourt, Edmond et Jules de, *Journal* (4 vols; Paris, 1878).
Graves, Robert, *Lawrence and the Arabs* (London, 1927).
Grosrichard, Alain, *Structure de serail* (Paris, 1979).
Haller, John, *Outcasts from Evolution* (Urbana, 1971).
Hellerstein, E., L. Hume and K. M. Offen (eds) *Victorian Women* (London, 1981).
Hering, Fanny Field, *Gérôme, his Life and Works* (Paris, 1911).
Hibbert, Christopher, *The Great Mutiny: India 1857* (London, 1978).
Hodgson, G., *The Life of James Elroy Flecker* (Oxford, 1925).
Hyam, Ronald, *Britain's Imperial Century* (London, 1976).
Islam, Shamsul, *Chronicles of the Raj* (London, 1979).
Jardine, Lisa, *Still Harping on Daughters* (London, 1983).

Jassim Ali, Muhsin, *Scheherazade in England* (Washington, 1981).
Jullian, Phillippe, *Les Orientalistes* (Fribourg, 1977).
Kedourie, Elie, *England and the Middle East* (London, 1956).
——, *Islam in the Modern World* (London, 1980).
Kiernan, V. G., *The Lords of Human Kind: European Attitudes towards the Outside World in the Imperial Age* (London, 1969).
Kimber, William, *Edward Lear in Greece* (London, 1965).
Kirkpatrick, B. J. (ed.) *A Catalogue of the Library of Sir Richard Burton* (London, 1978).
Knightley, Phillip and Colin Simson, *The Secret Lives of Lawrence of Arabia* (London, 1969).
Lacan, Jean, *Les Sarrazins dans le haut Moyen-Age Français* (Paris, 1965).
Lane-Poole, Stanley, *The Story of Cairo* (London, 1902).
Lapauze, Henri, *Ingres, sa vie et son oeuvre* (Paris, 1911).
Lawrence, A. W. (ed.) *T. E. Lawrence by His Friends* (London, 1937).
Lerner, Michael, *Pierre Loti* (New York, 1974).
Lewis, Archibald, *Naval Power and Trade in the Mediterranean (AD 500–1100)* (Princeton, 1951).
Le Yaounc, Colette, *L'Orient dans la poesie anglaise de l'époque romantique* (Paris, 1975).
Liddell Hart, B. H., *T. E. Lawrence in Arabia and After* (London, 1934).
Longford, Elizabeth, *A Pilgrimage of Passion: The Life of Wilfrid Scawen Blunt* (London, 1982).
Louca, Anwar, *Voyageurs et écrivains egyptiens en France au 19ième siècle* (Paris, 1970).
Lowes, J. L., *The Road to Xanadu* (Boston, 1927).
Mack, J. E., *A Prince of our Disorder: The Life of T. E. Lawrence* (Boston, 1976).
Marchand, Leslie, *The Athenaeum: A Mirror of Victorian Culture* (Chapel Hill, 1941).
Marcus, Stephen, *The Other Victorians* (London, 1966).
MacFarlane, Allen, *Witchcraft in Tudor and Stuart England* (London, 1970).
Melville, Lewis, *Life and Letters of William Beckford of Fonthill* (London, 1910).
Meryon, Charles, *Memoirs of Lady Hester Stanhope* (London, 1846).
Metlitzki, Dorothee, *The Matter of Araby in Medieval England* (New Haven, 1977).
Meyer, P., *Aléxandre le Grand dans la Littérature du Moyen Age* (Paris, 1886).
Monroe, Elizabeth, *Philby of Arabia* (London, 1973).
Mousa, Suleiman, *T. E. Lawrence: An Arab View* (New York, 1966).
Muir, P. H., *English Children's Books (1600–1900)* (London, 1956).
Nasir, Sari, *The Arabs and the English* (London, 1979).
Oliver, J. W., *The Life of William Beckford* (London, 1932).
Paden, W. D., *Tennyson in Egypt* (Kansas, 1942).
Penzer, Norman, *An Annotated Bibliography of Sir Richard Burton* (London, 1923).
Pichois, Claude, *Baudelaire: Etude et Témoignages* (Neuchatel, 1967).
Pope-Hennessey, *Monckton Milnes: The Flight of Youth* (London, 1963).
Praz, Mario, *The Romantic Agony* (London, 1970).
Qalamawi, Suheir, *Alf Laila wa Laila* (Cairo, 1959).
Quennel, Peter, *The Book of the Marvels of India* (London, 1928).
Rajna, P., *Le Fonti dell'Orlando Furioso* (Florence, 1900).
Roosevelt, Theodore, *The Winning of the West* (2 vols; New York, 1896).
Rose, Andrea, *Pre-Raphaelite Portraits* (London, 1981).

Said, Edward W., *Orientalism* (London, 1978).

Salhani, Yassin M., *Richard Burton: A Study of His Translations from the Arabic* Ph.D. Dissertation, University of St. Andrews, 1978.

Satow, Michael and Ray Desmond, *Railways of the Raj* (London, 1982).

Schwab, Raymond, *La Renaissance Orientale* (Paris, 1950).

Searight, Sarah, *The British in the Middle East* (London, 1979).

Smith, Byron Porter, *Islam in English Literature* (New York, 1939).

Southern, R. W., *Western Views of Islam in the Middle Ages* (Cambridge, Mass., 1980).

Stocking, George, *Race, Culture, and Evolution* (New York, 1968).

Taha Hussein, M., *Le Romantisme Français et l'Islam* (Beirut, 1962).

Taseer, M. D., *India and the Near East in English Literature from the Earliest Times to 1924* Ph.D. Dissertation, Cambridge University, 1936.

Thornton, A. P., *Doctrines of Imperialism* (London, 1965).

Tibbetts, G. R., *A Study of the Arabic Texts containing Material on South-East Asia* (London, 1979).

Tidrick, Kathryn, *Heart-Beguiling Araby* (Cambridge, 1981).

Tonguç, S., *The Saracens in the Middle English Romances* (London, 1958).

Waardenburg, Jean-Jacques, *L'Islam dans le Miroir de l'Occident* (Paris, 1963).

White, B., *Saracens and Crusaders* (London, 1969).

Williams, Raymond, *Marxism and Literature* (Oxford, 1977).

Wood, A. C., *History of the Levant Company* (London, 1964).

Wright, Thomas, *The Life of John Payne* (London, 1954).

Yarlott, Geoffrey, *Coleridge and the Abyssinian Maid* (London, 1967).

Ziadeh, Nicholas, *Al-Jughrafiya wal Rahalat 'ind al 'Arab* (Beirut, 1962).

Index